Go Lightly

LAURENCE KING

Published by Laurence King Publishing
361–373 City Road
London EC1V 1LR
United Kingdom
Tel: +44 20 7841 6900
Email: enquiries@laurenceking.com
www.laurenceking.com

A catalogue record for this book is available
from the British Library.

ISBN: 978-1-78627-892-0

Illustrations by Xuan Loc Xuan
Design: Alex Wright

Printed in China

Laurence King Publishing is committed to
ethical and sustainable production. We are
proud participants in the Book Chain Project®.
bookchainproject.com

Go Lightly

How to travel *without* hurting the planet

Nina Karnikowski

Laurence King Publishing

Contents

Dream Lightly   08

Pack Lightly   22

Move Lightly   36

Stay Lightly   50

Eat Lightly   64

Introduction

It was the day everything changed. A late spring morning in Australia, I was tapping away at my computer when an email popped up. 'An invitation to a 19-day private jet trip across Africa has arrived,' read my editor's message. 'Think you could take the assignment?' Three days with the gorillas in Rwanda, two days exploring Ethiopia's ancient rock-cut churches, three days visiting South Africa's winelands… it was the assignment of my dreams. Except that, as I went to respond, I realized my dreams had changed.

I had been a travel writer for eight years by then, criss-crossing the globe writing stories about everything from photography trips in Mongolia, to cruises in Antarctica, to rail journeys in India. I was passionate about sharing the joys of travel with curious readers, but I had been growing increasingly concerned about the impact my travels were having on our stressed planet. Certain memories – a plastic-covered island in Borneo, a distressed polar bear swimming away from our tourist boat in the Arctic – would not fade.

So I wrote back to my editor, declining the assignment. I realized it was a once-in-a-lifetime trip, but also that it was hugely carbon-heavy and would probably contribute little to local communities. That day I wrote another important email, this one to my publisher pitching this very book idea. I wanted to find out how I, and every traveller, could see the world in a much less harmful way.

A few months later coronavirus swept the globe. During lockdown, global carbon emissions decreased by as much as 17 per cent, the lowest level in 14 years, as we stopped flying and driving and consuming. Once our devastation about the loss of lives and livelihoods abated, we realized the pandemic could show us a cleaner, slower, more conscious travel world.

There is no time to lose when it comes to making changes, simply because so many more of us are travelling. The middle class is ballooning, there are more and bigger planes in our skies than ever before. Accommodation capacity has been massively increased by platforms such as Airbnb, and we stoke each other's wanderlust on social media. International arrivals went from 70 million in 1960 to about 1.4 billion today, a figure expected to reach 3 billion by 2050. An awful lot for this fragile planet of ours to handle.

But while the travel industry is responsible for an estimated 8 per cent of the world's carbon emissions, as well as degraded wilderness areas, overtouristed towns, the erosion of local cultures and more, it's also a lifeline. Tourism accounts for one in ten jobs, teaches tolerance and broadens world views. At its best, it can empower communities, support small social enterprises, and protect the wildest parts of our planet. And luckily, there are so many things we can all do to balance our curiosity with consciousness, and say yes to travel that conserves, educates and inspires more than it destroys. *Go Lightly* will help you do just that.

We can figure our way out of the mess we're in, but it requires a huge shift in collective consciousness. To start thinking of ourselves not as individuals, but as part of a giant human tribe uniting in the fight to save our precious home. And to dismantle everything we do, especially the way we travel, to make it more circular and regenerative. My guess is, the journey you'll take in rebuilding the way you travel will end up being the greatest adventure of your life so far. Mine certainly has been.

Dream
Lightly

Travelling more sustainably begins in
the dreaming stages. In those hours
spent scouring world maps, devouring
magazines, books, documentaries
and films. Superficial planning leads
to superficial experiences, but diving
deep into research makes journeys
richer and more meaningful, leaves
a cleaner footprint and can help
us recognize travel as the privilege
it is. From avoiding mass tourism
to choosing green companies and
clarifying motivations, this section
will help us discover where we want
to go and why.

Consider Under-Touristed Places

They're scenes to make any thinking traveller's blood run cold: thousands of tourists pouring off cruise ships and coaches in destinations such as Barcelona, Dubrovnik and Venice, where 260,000 locals deal with over 25 million tourists a year. Pre-coronavirus lockdown, they were being loved to death by tourists. Locals were pushed out of city centres, environments degraded, cultural identities lost, the very sights we were going to see ruined. While the travel hiatus restored balance to these destinations, we need to avoid returning to our destructive travel habits.

The wider we cast our travel nets, the better the chance of making our trips less stressful for communities and environments, and more unique and rewarding for us. My memories of big-ticket sights like the Louvre in Paris or Cambodia's Angkor Wat are mostly eclipsed by the heaving crowds; but the afternoons I spent getting lost in the backstreets of Mumbai are etched into my psyche forever.

Go Lightly Challenge

Instead of following the crowds, follow the threads of your own interests as you would at home. Into live music? Seek that. Love growing vegetables? Find local farmers and offer your services for a day. Get as niche and personal as possible.

What to Do

Get imaginative. Think beyond the places on travel magazine 'hot lists' and grabbing the best deal, instead seeking more off-track spots, and destinations that most need your tourist dollars. Consider using companies that specialize in helping you fall off the tourist map.

Searching 'alternatives to [popular destination]' is a good start, as is contacting locals on social media to ask about their favourite hidden places. They'll be easier and cheaper to book, you won't have to plan around the tourist rush, and locals will be happier to engage with you. Still desperate to visit a popular place? Consider travelling during the off-season, choosing outlying areas and staying for longer, to deepen both your connection to the place and your financial impact.

Choose 'Green' Companies

By prioritizing travel to countries with low-impact tourism policies that are serious about protecting natural resources, people and heritage, you're using your tourism dollars to endorse sustainability. Carbon-negative Bhutan, for example, caps tourist numbers and ensures that tourists spend a minimum of US $250 each day, while the Pacific archipelago of Palau asks visitors to sign a sustainable tourism pledge.

If you want to take some of the planning pressure off and enlist the help of a tour company, choose one that's eco-friendly and socially aware, remembering that if we, as consumers, refuse to invest our travel dollars into unsustainable companies, they'll have to adjust how they do business if they want to survive. This is about doing thorough research, then asking the right questions of management, or even the reservation person on the phone. Some to consider:

- How do your trips help protect and support wildlife and cultural heritage? In what ways are you having a positive impact on this destination?

- How big are your groups? Smaller groups usually have lighter impacts.

- Do you use locally owned and run hotels and restaurants, and employ local guides?

- What conservation measures are you taking for water, waste and energy?

There is an increasing number of eco-friendly travel companies on the market. Some of my favourites include: responsibletravel.com; intrepidtravel.com (carbon neutral since 2010); betterplacestravel.com (publishes the full impact of every trip they run); gadventures.com (calculates what percentage of spending from each trip stays in the local economy); and muchbetteradventures.com (aims to protect wild places through their trips).

Plan Slower Adventures

In our warp-speed modern world, when budget air travel has caused a rise in more frequent, shorter breaks, our trips often have superficial impacts, both in terms of our understanding of the places we visit, and the economic benefit to them. An antidote to this is to travel at a slower pace. Like so many things in the sustainability realm we need to pay attention to those who have gone before us. My parents spent six months driving through Europe in the 1970s, camping, picnicking and doing all the things I now aspire to do when I travel. And guess what? They *still* talk about that trip, 40 years later.

What to Do

- Take fewer but longer trips, storing up vacation days or waiting for a sabbatical or long-service leave so you can linger and forge real bonds with people you meet.

- Pick one place, not four, to visit in a week.

- Consider off-season travel, when there are fewer crowds and things are often cheaper.

- Savour the journey – those long train, van or boat trips – as much as the destination.

- Organize less, and keep yourself open to discovery.

We pack our travel itineraries to the brim because we're terrified we'll miss something. But what we're really missing is serendipity, and the simple ability to fall in love with our planet – the very thing we need to do if we are going to live in harmony with it, and create the change we want to see.

Travel Closer to Home

As someone who for years prioritized exploring the plains of Mongolia and the mountains of India over her own country, I understand the lure of the exotic. Choosing destinations closer to home, however, might be one of the best ways to lighten our carbon footprint.

What to Do

Visit unfamiliar neighbourhoods in your own town or city, exploring them with the same wide-eyed curiosity you would while visiting Morocco, Nepal or Kyrgyzstan. Another option is a 'microcation', taking the train to a nearby beach or forest for a few days. A powerful reset, without burning massive amounts of carbon.

If it is the exotic you crave, try drawing more of this into your life at home by listening to music and watching films and documentaries from the place you're dreaming of, eating at restaurants that serve food from there, taking a language course, attending events or exhibitions related to your desired destination, or visiting cultural hubs (Chinatown, Little Italy, Little India etc.) in your own city.

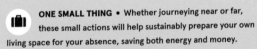

ONE SMALL THING • Whether journeying near or far, these small actions will help sustainably prepare your own living space for your absence, saving both energy and money.

- Eat, freeze and give away perishables.
- Unplug appliances.
- Consider renting out your car.
- Set the water heater and thermostat to 'vacation mode'.
- Turn off the water supply to the inside of the house.

Work Out Your 'Why'

Clarifying the purpose behind each journey will make them more satisfying, meaningful and memorable, will help us understand destinations better, will likely offer us knowledge that we can share back home, and can help us be a force for good in the places we visit. It's the perfect antidote to the 'going without thinking' movement and will make us think harder about what we're spending our travel dollars on.

To discover the intention behind your next adventure, try asking yourself these questions:

- Can my trip teach me how to be more sustainable at home? This could be anything from an off-grid multi-day hike to a conservation-focused road trip.

- Where can I go to learn more about my obsessions and interests? This could include language skills, or developing your love of history, art, surfing or sewing.

- Do I want to give back? Tread cautiously with volunteering, and remember that investing in locally owned businesses and conservation projects can often be the best way to give back.

- Can I learn a skill that will improve my life back home? Maybe you can hone your cooking skills, learn about permaculture, or deepen your meditation practice.

- Is there an aspect of my personal growth I'd like to work on? This could be a physical challenge, say a trek or mountain climb, or a spiritual quest, such as spending some time in a retreat.

Conscious Travel Hero
====

Elizabeth Becker

Journalist and author, on avoiding
mass tourism **elizabethbecker.com**

'We're all going to have to make hard sacrifices. Sustainable tourism requires a really strong change.'

When former *New York Times* and *Washington Post* correspondent Elizabeth Becker wrote *Overbooked: The Exploding Business of Travel and Tourism* in 2013, she was ahead of the curve. Overtourism is now a prominent issue and Becker continues to lead important conversations about it, everywhere from BBC World News to forums at George Washington University.

What does sustainable travel mean to you?

Something that tackles overtourism and the climate crisis. And it means a really strong change, by both the industry and consumers. We need to stop taking so many plane trips – two a year is a lot, anything else should be by train. Too many business trips are still taken that could be done with video conferencing. And we need to look at *why* we're travelling – if it's for Instagram, we have to change our ideas.

Your favourite green journey?

I know what green travel is because I'm of an age where that's the only kind of travel we used to do! We weren't travelling to be the stars of our own videos, we were going slowly and really getting to know a place. But my most recent favourite green journey was crossing the Atlantic from the US to France on the RMS *Queen Mary 2* ocean liner. We took the train to Bordeaux, one of Europe's greenest cities, where we rented an apartment and lived like locals for two months.

The biggest mistake you've made in terms of sustainable travel?

Not relying on a travel agent who understands sustainability. The first time I tried to organize a trip on my own it was a mess, and I have the highest respect now for good travel agents. Find a travel agent you like and who understands you and your concerns – by working with them, pretty soon you'll figure out how you can travel more sustainably in the future.

What is your utopian vision of the future of travel?

During this pandemic we glimpsed the damage overtourism has done. Without air travel, people from Los Angeles to Beijing saw clear skies. Wildlife reappeared. I would like to see measures to recover that momentum: one day a week with no air travel at all. Restrictions that prevent crowds from massing in wildlife parks. The list is long.

Elizabeth's tips to *Go Lightly*:

- Take fewer trips, but spend more time in each place. The more time you spend in a place, the more you respect the local environment, and the more the destination benefits.

- If the place you want to go is overtouristed, find an alternative. And instead of guidebook suggestions of sites to visit there, follow your own interests.

- As a traveller, think as a citizen, not a consumer. Treat a place as if it were your own and follow the rules.

The Hiking Trip

Hiking adventures are as close as the non-religious get to a pilgrimage. They are physical challenges that also often become spiritual ones, with many of us deciding to press the soles of our shoes to the soul of the world in order to rediscover our true north. No wonder books such as Cheryl Strayed's *Wild* (2012) and Jon Krakauer's *Into the Wild* (1996) are bestsellers – we're fascinated by the idea that we can walk our way back to ourselves.

In 2016 I trekked the remote Ausangate trail in Peru, which I chose as an alternative to overtouristed Machu Picchu, hiking along ragged snow-dusted peaks to the Rainbow Mountain. The trip became a pilgrimage of sorts; by going outside I found, as many hikers do, that I was actually going inside, where I was able to tap into hidden parts of myself.

Studies in Italy and Japan have shown that being immersed in nature makes our brains healthier, increases our attention span and creativity, and lowers blood pressure, heart rate and levels of the stress hormone cortisol. This is what the Japanese call *shinrin-yoku*, or forest bathing, which encourages us to slow down and soak up nature with all our senses – the smell of the plants and soil around us, the

soothing sight of greenery, the feel of the earth beneath our feet, the gentle murmur of the forest – helping us stay focused, mindful and present.

Being surrounded by a flourishing natural environment inspires us to feel awe for our planet. Research tells us that it's precisely this feeling of awe that tends to make us feel kinder and more generous, and encourages us to forgo our personal interests for those of others and the world. Exactly what is needed at this crucial moment in time.

Plan + Eco-Charge Your Hiking Trip

Route

If you discover a destination is popular, like the Camino de Santiago in Spain or the Appalachian Trail in the US, choose a quieter alternative for a lighter environmental impact (thehikinglife.com has some good ideas). Treks or hikes in your own part of the world are preferable.

Gear

The less gear you can take the better. For necessities such as tents, consider hiring or borrowing. If you are buying, try for second-hand, or choose consciously produced adventure brands such as patagonia.com (or their used clothing site wornwear.com), vaude.com or mammut.com, and eco products including feather-free sleeping bags and backpacks made from recycled PET bottles. Natural sunscreen and insect repellent are must-packs, so you're not leaching chemicals into waterways. If you're going somewhere cold, look for cruelty-free brands such as noize.com, which makes PETA-approved, fashion-forward vegan outerwear.

With Kids

If you have small kids, the right pram can be a lifesaver – one that zips up and keeps insects out, and turns into a bed so they can sleep for sections. Extra snacks and biodegradable nappies are important, as is packing a couple of books or toys. Keep kids engaged by having an end goal each day – hot springs or a waterfall, say. And start small, getting them familiar with shorter hikes, then working up to multi-days.

Accommodation

If you're camping, stick to defined sites. Otherwise, choose the most eco-friendly accommodation available – small, locally owned guesthouses, teahouses or lodges.

Entertainment

Download podcasts relating to the history and flora and fauna of your destination, and plant-identifying apps such as PlantSnap or PictureThis. Music from the place you're in will help get you through difficult sections of a hike.

Food

Make snacks such as energy balls and trail mix, using local food without loads of air miles. Pack biodegradable bags for waste, bring a high-capacity bottle or bladder for water, and take a purifier like a SteriPEN to easily refill.

Let it Be

Those pretty flowers might be an insect's or animal's habitat or dinner, so resist picking them; same with collecting stones and pieces of wood. Keep a comfortable distance from wild animals so you don't affect their behaviour, and stick to marked trails so you're not treading on any creature's habitat. Avoid walking along the edges of paths ('braiding'), which over time makes them wider; and collect any litter you find.

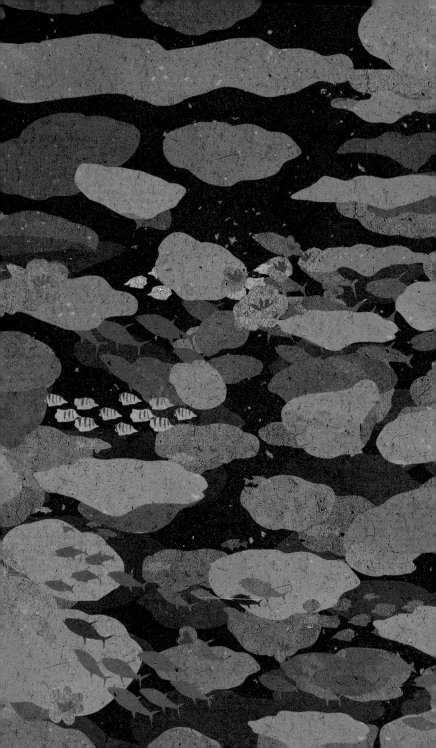

Pack Lightly

We've all been there. It's 11.00 PM the night before a big trip, and you've only just started throwing things into your suitcase. Packing more sustainably requires more planning and time – but trust me, your travels will be better for it. In this section we'll cover the basics of packing lightly, which reusables to take so you can be plastic-free, what 'packing with purpose' means, and more.

Travel with Less

Packing less is better for the planet – the heavier your bag, the heavier the plane and the more fuel that plane needs. It's also better for your wallet (no extra luggage fees) and, unencumbered by excess stuff, you'll be better able to squeeze your bag on top of that bus in India, or fit in that final beach swim in Costa Rica, knowing that packing will take less time.

Light Packing Tips

- **Don't buy a holiday wardrobe. Fashion is the planet's second-largest polluter, and we now consume 80 *billion* pieces of clothing each year. Work with what you've got or borrow from friends if you need something specific (I often use social media to do call-outs for this). If you do need to buy, choose second-hand, or good quality timeless pieces and sustainable brands.**

- **Pack in advance. Light packing takes time and energy, so start a few days before you depart, leaving time to edit out surplus items.**

- **Consider a backpack. You'll be more aware of superfluous weight. Trust me, I backpacked around Europe with 25 kilos (55 pounds) on my back – it was 14 years ago and I still remember the pain.**

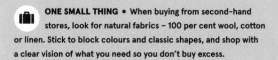

ONE SMALL THING • When buying from second-hand stores, look for natural fabrics – 100 per cent wool, cotton or linen. Stick to block colours and classic shapes, and shop with a clear vision of what you need so you don't buy excess.

- Choose a 'capsule wardrobe'. Basics in durable fabrics such as denim or linen that require minimal washing.

- Pack multi-functional items. A sarong that doubles as a scarf, sandals you can use as hiking shoes, etc.

- Take a sewing kit. Repair and care for your things. If sewing isn't your forte, take them to an alterationist.

Go Plastic-Free

Almost every piece of plastic ever made is still on the planet in some form, including 70 billion or so plastic bottles; and about 8 million tons of plastic is dumped into our oceans each year. Unless we take extreme action now, scientists say the amount of plastic in our oceans will triple by 2030. I find these figures hugely depressing too, but let's use them to fuel action, and as a reminder of what's at stake when it comes to accepting plastic bottles, bags and straws (disposable bioplastics should be avoided too; they present their own challenges). These sneaky single-use plastics can mostly be easily avoided by packing some sustainable travel accessories. There's a detailed list on page 140, but three of my favourites are:

- Insulated water bottle, which doubles as a reusable cup.

- Stainless-steel reusable food container.

- Linen or hemp tote for shopping or collecting trash.

Go Lightly Challenge

Try accepting as little single-use plastic (SUP) as possible on your next adventure, carrying reusables in your day bag and always requesting your food to come without plastic. If you manage to go a whole trip without accepting a single plastic straw, bottle, cup or other SUP, treat yourself. You can also turn this into a competition with the people you're travelling with – maybe the loser has to shout the others dinner on the final night.

Avoid cotton: the creation of one cotton T-shirt uses 2,700 litres (590 gallons) of water, or as much as you might drink in three years.

If a hotel puts plastic water bottles in your room, ask for a reusable glass one instead and a communal refill station (if you're ever unsure that water is potable, use a SteriPEN or similar water purifier), as well as for alternatives to plastic cups and miniature plastic toiletry bottles.

And don't get your suitcase plastic-wrapped at the airport. Invest in a good lock if you're worried about security, and let go of the need to have a scratch-free suitcase.

For other plastic-free and zero-waste solutions, for travel or otherwise, check out blogs such as trashisfortossers.com and goingzerowaste.com.

Dress Sensitively

Before you start packing, research local customs and beliefs and learn how to dress in a way that's culturally appropriate for your destination. The last thing we want to do is offend our hosts, and by that, I mean every citizen of the country we're visiting.

I cringe when I look back at photos of my 23-year-old self in Egypt, wearing tiny denim shorts at the Great Pyramid of

> **ONE SMALL THING** • Read books and news stories about your destination, listen to music and watch films and documentaries made there. Getting well informed politically, culturally and ecologically extends the life of your trip, helps you become more respectful of the land and its people, and makes for richer experiences.

Giza. I remember defiantly asserting I was free to dress how I pleased, I didn't agree that women should have to cover up and so I refused to. Thank goodness we learn from our mistakes.

Respecting local customs, whether we agree with them or not, is crucial. If you're visiting a culture where women don't reveal their hair, arms and legs, you should do the same. If you invited someone to your house and asked them to take their shoes off but they refused, you'd be offended, right? It's the same thing when we're travelling abroad. Always respect the locals' wishes – and if in doubt, err on the side of conservative.

Pack with Purpose

Another benefit of packing light is that there'll be extra room in your backpack or suitcase to bring supplies that might benefit the people you're visiting. Whether you're headed to Asia or North America, Africa or Europe, Central or South America, you'll find communities all around the world that are in need.

'Need' is the key word here, and it's critically important to research what a community *really* requires, so they're not left with unwanted or unnecessary things that they'll then be obliged to dispose of. Remember that this isn't a feel-good exercise or part of our own spiritual fulfilment, but about alleviating poverty and really trying to help.

Even if we have done a lot of research and have spent a good chunk of time in a country, we're unlikely to have a deep enough understanding of the local way of life to know exactly what supplies would be useful, so it's helpful to use a non-profit such as packforapurpose.org which specializes in exactly this. Travellers can search by country and region, and source a list of essentials that different communities around the globe have said they need (educational and medical supplies, usually) and instructions for where donations can be dropped off. Brilliant. If you're travelling with a responsible travel company, they'll be able to offer advice on this too.

Five Favourite Books for More Conscious Adventures

- *The Soul of Place* (2015) by Linda Lappin – how to write about place

- *The Tao of Travel* (2011) by Paul Theroux – on the deeper meaning of our travels

- *The Art of Travel* (2002) by Alain de Botton – on how to deepen our voyages

- *Traveling Souls* (1999) by Brian Bouldrey (ed.) – essays on travel as pilgrimage

- *On Photography* (1977) by Susan Sontag – a philosophical look at why we photograph

Learn the Language

If one of our ultimate aims for travel is to get to know a destination intimately, and one of the best ways of doing that is by talking to people, then consider making an effort to learn the local language before leaving home.

It's a sign of respect locals will appreciate – I never feel more obnoxious than when I find myself expecting to be understood simply because I'm speaking English. You'll create more authentic connections, and seeing a taxi driver's or shopkeeper's face light up when you know how to say hello to them in their own language is a huge reward in itself.

Ideas for Language Learning

- Sign up for language classes, either before leaving or at the destination.

- Take an online course, using sites like michelthomas.com or busuu.com.

- Download a translation app – Duolingo and Memrise are easy, fun and free.

- Learn key phrases by heart. When a friend recently went to Japan she learned to say, 'What's your favourite?' and 'Please choose for me' – she always got the best things on the menu, and it started great interactions with locals. 'Can I please have that without plastic?' is another good one to learn.

- Packing cards written with key phrases, which you can show to locals, helps. Could be seen as overkill, but people are usually delighted you have made an effort.

Conscious Travel Hero

Tanya Streeter

Free diver and environmentalist,
on sustainable travel with kids

plasticoceans.uk • @tanyastreeter

'Kids are so open to doing things the right way, if they're shown.'

As one of the world's best free divers, Tanya Streeter is as
fearless as they come, diving to depths of up to 160 metres
(525 feet) on one breath. Mother of two, she is acutely aware
of the impact climate change and pollution are having on
our seas. She gives TED talks on the topic and features in
environmental documentaries such as *A Plastic Ocean* (2016).

When did you first realize what a dire state our oceans are in?

I was born in the Cayman Islands, and the sea was where I
felt most comfortable and protected. I remember being nine
and free diving to scuba divers who were grabbing coral,
and waving my finger at them like, 'don't touch!' I remember
diving to pick up tourists' sunglasses and plastic cups.
In my early twenties when I started to dive competitively
I realized this is a huge problem, this was not this bad when
I was a child. I'm 47 now, and I've seen whole ecosystems
negatively affected by pollution and human impact.

What does sustainable travel mean to you?

It means making sure we don't negatively impact the people
who call the places we visit home, which is especially

important to me because I felt so negatively impacted by tourists. It means spending more time in destinations and making sure your money is going into the local economy.

Your favourite green journey?

Shooting *A Plastic Ocean* was most impactful. Every time I came home, I'd change something about the way my family and I were living. The 'green' journey I'm taking with my family thanks to *Plastic Ocean* is the one that trumps all others.

One of the most sustainable things you've done on a trip?

I love using public transportation, and doing things the way locals do. I took my 12-year-old, Tilly, to Moscow recently because my girlfriend was launching to the space station from Kazakhstan; Tilly navigated the metro for us. While other things will fade from our Moscow experience, rubbing shoulders with locals on the metro will stick.

The biggest mistake you've made in terms of sustainable travel?

Begging my mum to let me swim with captive dolphins. But it led me to know that any captive animal is not behaving naturally. I said it through my athletic career: my successes hardly taught me anything – my failures taught me so much.

Tanya's tips to *Go Lightly*:

- Do little things and urge others to do so. Think of the meme: 'It's just one plastic straw… said 8 billion people.'

- Wash your own clothes. Hotel laundries equate to water and energy waste, so I wash mine with me in the shower.

- Walk everywhere. It's healthy for you and the planet, and you see, feel and experience more.

The Biking Expedition

A whoosh, a whiz – then fresh air, freedom, and the open road. Whether it's a weekend jaunt or an epic overseas adventure, travelling by bike is one of the most gratifying and immersive ways to travel. You can see the world while staying fit and leaving the lightest of ecological wheelprints.

Picture yourself cycling down the backroads of an off-piste European city for a week, traversing open countryside upholstered with wildflowers, or freewheeling along dirt tracks, nothing but the forest canopy or the empty blue sky above your head. Sheer, unadulterated joy and freedom.

Bikes really are one of the most liberating forms of transport ever invented. Perched on your two-wheeled steed, you can explore a place at your speed, while using all of your senses to really get to know the destination. Biking trips allow you to smell, hear and feel it all – the wind and sun on your face, the moist scent of earth and wild grasses, the sounds of the birds as you zip along dusty trails. In the new era of social distancing, bikes have the added benefit of getting you around without needing to worry about spreading germs.

Biking is a form of transport that unfurls you. Out there on the road, your mind unspools. By the day's end, you can

feel as if you've sorted your whole life out in your head. Cycling trips are also likely to include some challenges, which ultimately bring you closer to both yourself and your travel companions. And once you return home, you will hopefully be encouraged to jump on your bike more often in everyday life, which just might be the best part of all.

Plan + Eco-Charge Your Biking Expedition

Choose Your Style

After low hassle and high comfort, with gear support, showers and warm beds each night and zero need to deal with logistical faff yourself? Prefer more of a challenge, camping and carrying everything on your bike? Dreaming of going solo, or travelling in a small group? Want to pedal through towns to learn about culture; through rural areas, stopping at farms to learn about the slow food movement; or through wilderness where you're unlikely to encounter other humans for days at a time? It's completely up to you.

Distance

Whatever your fitness level, try to keep the kilometres travelled relatively low each day, so you can soak up the scenery and stop for rests, picnics or exploring. Think about setting goals like learning about the areas you're passing through, or meeting interesting new people. Three to four hours of cycling a day is plenty (the number of kilometres covered will depend on the terrain, hills, weather etc.). Factor in rest days (at least one a week is recommended to let your body recover) and spare time for getting lost, breaking down, or simply following your curiosity.

Extra Support

Not sure your fitness is up to it? Consider an e-bike, which can be ridden as a regular bike but switched into electric mode for when you need help. Scooters and motorbikes are another option, although they are more carbon-heavy.

Gear

Other than your trusty bike, essentials include panniers, a good helmet (consider a bamboo option) and a repair kit – again, hire or borrow as much as possible. If it's your first cycling trip and you need activewear, choose more sustainable companies such as Atayne, whose quick-drying products are made from post-consumer plastic bottles, or OORR, which crafts its jerseys partly from coffee grounds enabling them to dry supposedly 50 per cent faster. Consider borrowing an action camera from friends to strap on your handlebars if you want to document hands-free.

With Kids

Biking trips are an excellent way for families to slow down and connect, while keeping kids active. For babies and young children, invest in a second-hand bike seat or zip-up weather-proof trailer stocked with crayons and paper, or for older kids a trailercycle (a small half-bike that attaches to yours) so they can pedal when they're feeling strong, or just sit back and enjoy the ride. If they're over 12, consider a tandem bike. Stop every hour to let the kids play and explore, and take a camera to keep them occupied. Ease into it with simple trips – to a campsite a couple of hours' ride from home, say – and work towards weekend or week-long trips.

Entertainment

Podcasts about the history of your destination are great for whiling away the hours, and music helps with tough climbs.

Move Lightly

For a long time I turned a blind eye to the impact the dozens of flights I was taking each year had on the planet. Now, thanks to wake-up calls from the likes of Greta Thunberg and Extinction Rebellion, I know that three-quarters of the CO_2 emissions from tourism are transport-related. Luckily, there are many things we can do to lighten our impact, such as using public transport, prioritizing train travel, offsetting our carbon emissions, and more.

Fly Smarter

Before COVID, many of us were feeling *flygskam* ('flight shame'), knowing air travel generated around 2.5 per cent of global carbon emissions. That percentage has diminished, but if we return to business as usual passenger numbers are set to double in twenty years, with the International Air Transport Association predicting 8.2 billion passengers annually by 2037. We have to start minimizing. Keep in mind this gruesome fact from David Wallace-Wells's *The Uninhabitable Earth* (2019): every plane seat from New York to London melts another 3 square metres (32 square feet) of Arctic ice, and burns the same amount of carbon as eight months of driving.

What to Do

Planes that don't use jet fuel are still a long way off, so we simply need to fly less, taking fewer but longer trips. And question whether a series of Skype meetings couldn't substitute that business trip.

Buying carbon offsets is another option. Visit a site such as native.eco or climatecare.org and calculate the emissions your flight produces (ground travel and food can also be included), then pay the offset company to invest in offsetting projects.

While offsets are better than nothing, they can take years or decades to make a difference (particularly tree planting), and critics say they discourage industry investment into cleaner technologies. I usually choose offset schemes that invest in clean-energy projects, such as distributing efficient cooking stoves or capturing methane at landfill sites, since they're quicker to take effect and offer social benefits.

Extra Things to Do

- Book the most direct route, since taking off and landing burns the most fuel.

- Fly economy. Business and first-class seats take up more space, so fewer people can fit on each flight.

- Prioritize airlines that use biofuels or more fuel-efficient and younger planes, such as Air New Zealand (in the past decade they have reduced their emissions by almost 22 per cent) and easyJet (the world's first airline to operate net-zero carbon flights).

- Combine work trips with holidays to get more from your flight.

- If you fly regularly, adjust emissions in other areas. I often fly for work, so I committed to giving up beef and to buying no new clothes for half of each year.

Clip Your Wings

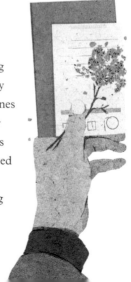

The Swedes have coined another fantastic term, *tagskryt* or 'train bragging', something else we might consider embracing. Not only do trains produce fewer emissions than planes (up to 50 per cent less fuel than a plane for a similar journey) and other options such as ferries or cars, those emissions aren't released directly into the upper atmosphere.

Some impressive green headway is being made with trains too, especially in Europe.

In early 2020, Eurostar started planting a tree for every train it operates, while electric trains in the Netherlands are powered completely by wind energy.

The benefits of rail travel aren't just environmental, though. There's a wonderful sense of nostalgia to it, whether you're being transported back to a more elegant age of travel on a luxury train in India, or whizzing through Japan on the futuristic, high-speed Shinkansen (head to page 46 for more on train travel).

Build more Train Travel into Your Trips

- Choose destinations with excellent rail networks, such as Germany, Japan, France and China.

- Consider buying a rail pass – like an Amtrak rail pass in the US, or a Eurail pass in Europe – which offers discounted rates for passes covering multiple journeys.

- If you're travelling in cities, use trains and subways to get around instead of cabs. They'll help you understand the local life better, and you'll discover parts of the city you otherwise wouldn't have.

BYO Transit Meals

Water served in plastic cups or bottles, nuts or chips in little plastic packets, meals served in plastic containers with plastic cutlery wrapped in plastic packaging… transit meals can be plastic tsunamis.

Bringing your own (BYO) reusable water bottle and bamboo cutlery can certainly help you avoid these devilish single-use plastics, but the best approach could be bringing your own transit meals and snacks in reusable containers (you can now buy ones that are set up like bento boxes, with different sections for various foods, perfect for travel), letting airline staff know why you're doing it.

You can bring your own food on to a plane, provided you eat any fruits and vegetables before you get to your destination in case there are quarantine and customs regulations, and that your food fits within the liquid restrictions if you're flying internationally. Hot tip: avoid soup and yoghurt. Oh, and anything that will stink out the cabin for your fellow travellers – maybe leave the curried egg sandwiches at home.

Consider taking leftovers that would otherwise be tossed out – the containers you carry them in will be handy for things like leftovers and snacks when you get to your destination.

Some Foods that Travel Well

- **Trail mix**
- **Crackers**
- **Fresh-cut fruit**
- **Salads**
- **Sandwiches**
- **Carrot sticks**

Bringing your own food has the added benefits of ensuring you're eating healthy, fresh food (avoiding highly salted and processed plane food) and that you can eat whenever you want (especially great if you're travelling with kids).

Pick Pedals or Feet

You've slowed your travels down so you don't need to jet around an entire country in ten days, but you still want to be mobile once you get there. How do you decide what the most sustainable approach is?

There are trains, coaches and buses, of course, all of which will give you an insight into local life, while letting you see more of the landscape. If you want to follow your own schedule, consider hiring a car (electric or hybrid, if they're available) or motorbike. There are now terrific car-sharing companies like zipcar.com or liftshare.com, which let you hire cars by the hour or day without using a middleman.

Hitchhiking is another option in certain parts of the world. There are some fantastic apps for safe and super-affordable ride sharing, such as Hitchhiker Carpooling and Waze Carpool for long distances. UberPool also lets you split your Uber ride with other travellers, for shorter trips.

For maximum eco-cred, choose biking, e-biking or walking, if you feel safe and comfortable enough to do them in your destination. Not only do these cause zero emissions, they also keep you fit and put you in the centre of the action. Some of my favourite trips have been along these lines – snowshoeing between rural towns in Hokkaido in northern Japan, trekking between medieval villages in Georgia's remote Svaneti region, or whizzing along palm-lined trails on a pushbike in Goa, India.

Cruise Thoughtfully

The cruise industry is notorious for its poor environmental practices. Mega-ships carrying thousands of passengers have monstrous environmental impacts, encompassing everything from air, water and noise pollution to erosion caused by their powerful wakes. They can also lead to superficial experiences, minimal financial benefit for local economies because of the short amount of time spent in each destination, and chronic overtouristing.

Having said this, seeing a country by water can be a terrific way of travelling, especially if you have limited mobility, provided you do it right. Here are some guidelines:

- Pick smaller ships with no more than 250 passengers (the biggest cruise ship in the world, the *Symphony of the Seas*, carries 6,680 guests and 2,200 crew), since most use cleaner marine gas oil rather than fuel oil. As with planes, the newer the ship, the more energy-efficient and eco-sensitive it's likely to be.

- Find cruises that give you time onshore to eat in restaurants and explore in more meaningful ways.

- Choose companies that prioritize sustainability. For example, Virgin Voyages has no single-use plastics on board and focuses on waste and water recycling, while Peregrine Adventures offers carbon neutral cruises.

- If you're visiting fragile environments such as the Galapagos Islands or Antarctica, choose a company that's affiliated with an environmental regulator.

Go Lightly Challenge

For your next trip, try to keep your carbon emissions as low as possible (scientists say individual annual emissions need to be kept below 5 tons a year to prevent dangerous climate change). This will inspire you to travel by foot, stay in homes rather than hotels, travel closer to home and more.

The better option though, if you're keen on an ecological nautical adventure, is choosing sailing over cruising. If you charter a yacht or sailboat, your carbon footprint will be much lighter, you'll be able to travel on your own schedule, and you can visit the more remote villages and unspoilt beaches that cruise ships can't access. You can also stay in places longer, making a more meaningful contribution to the local economy and creating more distinctive memories.

Conscious Travel Hero
_____

Céline Cousteau

Conservationist and filmmaker,
on travelling with intent

celinecousteau.com • @celinecousteau

'We used to think several generations ahead. We need to return to that.'

Granddaughter of the French explorer and conservationist Jacques Cousteau, Céline Cousteau creates documentary films with her company CauseCentric Productions. She advocates for connecting people and the environment, and is an ambassador for the TreadRight Foundation.

What does sustainable travel mean to you?

Doing the best you can with every choice you make, from the companies and airlines you travel with to whether you need to go as far as you're going to find what you're looking for.

How can we make our travels mean more?

Choose companies that give back, or volunteer at sustainable farms or reputable animal rescues. You'll connect to people who are moving the needle, and come back enriched.

Your favourite green journey?

A recent trip to Atalaia, the border town with the Javari indigenous territory I work in in the Brazilian Amazon. I got to show the Javari the film they asked me to make for them and one of them told me, 'Céline, your film has saved lives.' Having them tell me 'your work matters to us' is what I needed to wake up my warrior spirit each morning and keep going. While the Amazon is my heart place, it's also one of the hardest places to go because the stories are heartbreaking. But I come back so grateful for the life I lead, with a reinvigorated energy to fight harder.

The biggest mistake you've made in terms of sustainable travel?
It's something I've had to resist doing. If you see a wild animal in a market and you want to buy it and set it free, you shouldn't, because you're contributing to the economy that creates that problem. You need to attack higher up.

The biggest change that needs to happen in travel?
Once you start fixing how you see this world, you start fixing everything you do. A glaciologist said to me, 'Unfortunately human beings don't react until our backs are against the wall, and when it comes to climate change, that's too late.' So it's also about thinking preventatively – thinking about our consumption now, our travel now, our behaviour towards other people now. My mum tells a story of a chief in an Amazonian village who pointed to a tree he planted and said, 'Someday that tree will make a great canoe. Not for me, not for my son, not for my grandson – maybe my grandson's son or his grandson.' Let's go back to that thinking. That matters.

Céline's tips to *Go Lightly*:

- Assess whether your travel is really necessary.

- Ask: is my travel going to benefit somebody other than me?

- Always travel with reusables. Don't count on other people to do it right, do it right yourself.

The Train Journey

Whether the train you're on is plush or primitive, speedy or slow, chaotic or calming, there's an undeniable romance to long-distance rail travel. Rocking back and forth in your cabin, listening to the click-clack of the wheels and watching the landscape unfold outside your window, you're transported to a different era of travel. A less carbon-heavy era, but also a more charming, enriching and exciting one.

Slow travel celebrates the journey as much as the destination, and nowhere is this more apparent than on a train. As you watch the outside world rushing past your window, you can also explore a new world inside as you wander through the carriages. People are usually more relaxed and open to getting to know each other on trains, so you can chat to fellow travellers, trade travel stories and learn about their home countries, and also pick up insider tips and accommodation options off the tourist trail for your destination. Inside a train you (and your kids, if you have them) aren't stuck in your seat for endless periods, enhancing your sense of freedom and stoking your explorer's spirit.

Mood is a key component of travel, and trains get things off to a good start in that respect, too. With no waiting at

airports, no long check-in, security and boarding lines, and none of the rage-inducing traffic involved in road travel, trains are almost guaranteed to put you in a positive frame of mind for your adventure. You're in charge of your own baggage so there's less chance of losing it, and trains usually deposit you right in the centre of the action so you don't have to waste money on taxis going to and from remote airports. Because they're less dependent on weather than planes, they're more reliable, too.

Train travel also has less impact on our bodies, without jet lag or the drops in cabin pressure and altitude that can leave you feeling bloated and lead to poor circulation. With the ability to roam around and jump out for the occasional station stop, you often alight from a train feeling just as good as when you got on, and immediately ready for adventure.

Plan + Eco-Charge Your Train Journey

Go Green

Not all trains are created equal. You'll obviously be limited to the options available in your destination, but where possible opt for electric trains, trains powered by wind energy, and companies that prioritize carbon offsetting. Take this into consideration whether you're taking a multi-day, high-end sleeper train journey, or simply using a train to travel between places.

Food + Drink

If you can order a meal served on actual plates with cutlery and glasses, that's usually the greenest option and will give you an insight into the culinary culture of the place you're

travelling through. If it's a BYO situation, opt for food with
the least amount of packaging and bring extra. Sharing food
is a terrific way to bond with other passengers.

Entertainment

With someone else doing the driving and navigating,
you'll be free to eat, nap, write, read, look out at the passing
scenery or wander around whenever you please. Bring a
good novel or non-fiction book about the destination you're
travelling through to get you in the mood, a journal to reflect
on the experience, and if you can't do without some screen
time (although train travel is a great opportunity for a digital
detox), consider a documentary or film about the destination
you're travelling in. Playing cards is another fun way to
connect with other passengers, especially since it doesn't
require advanced language skills.

Avoiding Theft

If you're not unpacking in a cabin for multiple days of train
travel, always pack a separate small backpack or duffel with
valuables, lock it with a padlock and keep it with you at all
times. It can even double as a pillow for catnaps.

Choosing Your Seat

Window seats are always best so you can maximize your
views of the landscape. If you can afford it, it's worth
spending a bit more on a sleeper compartment (especially
if you're saving on overnight accommodation) so you can
stretch out and get a good night's sleep. Bring an eye mask,
silicone earplugs and a blanket (I often bring an oversized
scarf for this) to keep cosy, and remember to set an alarm
to make sure you don't miss your stop.

Stay Lightly

According to the UN's World Tourism Organization, just 5 per cent of money spent by tourists actually stays in the local community. Shocking, but true. So when it comes to accommodation, the most important factor is choosing stays that inject money directly back into the local economy, avoiding foreign-owned hotel chains and rentals. Instead, we can support small-scale businesses and lodgings, including bed and breakfasts, homestays, farm stays, camping, and more.

Lodge Mindfully

To make sure your hard-earned travel dollars are being funnelled back into the country you're visiting, choose hotels that are locally owned. The smaller the hotel, the more likely it is to be owned and staffed by locals. These also usually produce much less rubbish and pollution than big resorts, and help you experience the destination in a more authentic way – consider how different a trip to Tokyo would be if you stayed in a high-rise international hotel chain, compared to a traditional ryokan inn.

Look for stays that will give you access to local communities. One of my favourite hotels is the 20-room Abode in Mumbai – it's a heritage building filled with local artisan work like hand-crafted tiles, salvaged furniture and hand-painted signs, is staffed entirely by locals including female taxi drivers and blind masseuses, and it's right in the centre of the action.

Look for Hotels that:

- Use renewable energies, like solar and wind power.

- Find innovative ways to reduce energy demands.

- Participate in sustainable community projects.

- Are sensitive to an area's environmental needs (minimizing water use in drought-prone areas, say).

- Are built with sustainable or salvaged materials.

- Are accessible for everyone, regardless of their age or physical challenges. Inclusivity should be rewarded.

Beware Greenwashing

Greenwashing happens throughout the travel world. An example is those notes hotels place in rooms telling you to reuse your towel, while they make little effort elsewhere to reduce water or energy consumption. Look closely at the claims hotels are making to be 'sustainable' or 'green'. If you want to make sure these claims have legs, pick up the phone and ask the right questions.

Some Questions to Ask

- I read on your website that you're sustainable: can you please tell me how?

- Do you have a recycling or composting programme?

- What do you do with your grey water?

- Do you employ locals or support the community?

- Is your food locally sourced?

Alternatively, hand the research over to the professionals and use a green accommodation search engine. Ecobnb.com focuses on reducing CO_2 emissions and enriching local communities and covers organic farmhouses, glamping and more; bookdifferent.com ensures that sustainability claims are checked by third parties and calculates carbon footprints; TripAdvisor's GreenLeaders Programme covers hotels and B&Bs committed to practices such as electric car charging.

I also often search for sustainability- or conservation-focused stories written about destinations I'm visiting in trusted magazines such as nationalgeographic.com, smithsonianmag.com or getlostmagazine.com, or sites such as sustainabletravel.org or traveltochangetheworld.com.

Consider Hotel Alternatives

Bed + Breakfasts

Usually owned by locals, and giving you a great opportunity to connect with your hosts over a lazy breakfast. House-sharing sites such as Airbnb can also be good, but these aren't yet well regulated and can disrupt local housing markets and inflate rents, forcing locals out. Before booking, check whether there's a shortage of housing for locals in that region, and how short-term rentals are regulated there.

Eco-Friendly Hostels

There are loads all around the world; just search 'eco-friendly hostel in [your destination]' and you're likely to find one. Hostels put you in direct contact with other travellers, often run great eco tours, are super-affordable and are becoming more design-savvy by the day.

House-Swapping + House-Sitting

Sites such as lovehomeswap.com or homeexchange.com allow like-minded travellers to exchange stays in each other's homes, while sites such as trustedhousesitters.com connect animal lovers to locals who need their home and pets looked after while they're away, in exchange for a free stay at their place.

Homestays

For an even deeper experience, homestays have you living under the same roof as locals, so you can learn about their way of life first-hand, with sites such as homestay.com connecting guests to local hosts.

WWOOFing

For a small annual fee, members of wwoofinternational.org (World Wide Opportunities on Organic Farms) can stay on farms, vineyards, gardens and smallholdings around the world for free, helping hosts with farming tasks in exchange for accommodation, food and knowledge.

Agri-Tourism

Chic versions of WWOOFing, basically. Like Cook the Farm (see annatascalanza.com), a two-month cooking course held at a Sicilian vineyard where travellers learn to prune vines, grind wheat and make cheese; or the five-day Kitchen on the Edge of the World hotel in Norway (holmenlofoten.no), where guests fish, hike, hunt and gather food with a TV chef.

Historic Buildings

Landmarktrust.org.uk, a British building conservation charity, rescues historic buildings for travellers to rent, including a pineapple-shaped 1700s summerhouse in Scotland, and a cottage on a medieval abbey site near Portofino, Italy.

Embrace Camping or Vanning

You don't get much more eco-friendly than camping. You're having minimal impact on the Earth; and if you wild camp you're dealing with all your own waste, which means you're more mindful of how much you produce. You're also completely at one with the wilderness, sleeping under the stars and cooking meals over an open fire. Check local regulations, as wild camping is not permitted everywhere, and be very careful to extinguish fires safely.

Aside from also being one of the most economical choices of getaway, camping strips you back to the bare essentials, which helps you slow down and tune in.

If you're craving nature immersion but don't want to give up your creature comforts, try glamping – from geodesic domes in Chile to luxury safari tents in East Africa, from bell tents in the Australian bush to transparent 'bubble tents' in France. I stayed in a locally owned and run Bedouin camp in Jordan's Wadi Rum desert a few years ago, sleeping in a traditional black-and-white goat-hair tent tucked beneath soaring cliffs. It was one of the most memorable stays of my travelling life.

Travelling by campervan, RV or motorhome is another excellent option. You don't have to pack up constantly or organize transport between destinations. Minimalism is still key here – this is a chance to go fuss-free.

Go Lightly Challenge

During your next trip, try taking all non-compostable rubbish you generate home with you. It will make you look at packaging in a whole new light, and make you reconsider the rubbish you're dumping on local communities when you travel.

Do the Small Things

Whether you're staying in a five-star hotel, a tented eco lodge, a campsite, a homestay, a van or a yurt, small tweaks can make your stay greener.

- In a hotel, ask staff to please not clean your room every day, to save energy and water (especially important in places experiencing water shortages, like Cape Town in South Africa or Oaxaca in Mexico).

- Bring your own toiletries. It's horrific to consider the millions of tiny plastic bottles hotels around the world go through in a day. Request large containers of soap and shampoo to be fixed to the bathroom wall instead.

- Use lights and air-conditioning sparingly, and turn them off when you leave your room.

- If the coffee machine in your room uses pods, check whether the pods are compostable or biodegradable before using. Most are only recyclable (like Nespresso) and billions pour into landfill each year. Ask hotels to switch to a compostable or biodegradable brand.

- Decline the paper brochures and maps many hotels offer. Take a snap on your phone instead.

- Leave the bottled water in your room and have your own bottle filled with filtered water instead. Ask for jugs of filtered water to replace the bottled water, too.

If any of this comes across as 'making a fuss', great, because it will encourage hotels to adopt more eco-friendly solutions.

Marit Miners

Co-founder of Misool Eco Resort,
on travelling to create change

misool.info • @misool.resort

'Research before booking, to ensure the operator's values align with yours.'

Husband and wife team Marit and Andrew Miners are the visionaries behind Misool, one of the world's most highly regarded eco resorts, set in remote Raja Ampat in West Papua, Indonesia. The Miners built Misool on the site of an abandoned shark-finning camp, and it provides sustainable employment opportunities for the local community. It also funds their conservation initiatives, including the Misool Marine Reserve, which employs 15 local rangers.

What does sustainable travel mean to you?
Being a conscious consumer. Travel, when it's done intelligently and with care, has the power to connect people in meaningful ways with other cultures, environments and ecosystems. It has the power to transform 'them' into 'us'.

Your favourite green journey?
Visiting orangutans in the wild in Borneo. I was already aware of the catastrophic effect of palm oil cultivation on wildlife, biodiversity and CO_2 emissions, but making eye contact with these primates which are so like our own species moved me in a totally unexpected way. Their

existence is under threat because their human cousins demand cheap biscuits and margarine. Thanks to that journey, I'm dedicated to eradicating palm oil from my family's life.

The biggest mistake you've made in terms of sustainable travel?

I've ended up in places that were painfully greenwashed. We've all seen that self-congratulatory signage in hotels about not washing towels every day, but that should be standard. I learned that it's critical to do the research before booking.

The biggest change that needs to happen in travel?

The first is addressing overtourism and the struggle to maintain wild places. We need bold and decisive action from lawmakers to protect wilderness, and from travellers who may inadvertently love the wilderness to death. The second is the carbon emissions produced by the travel industry. How can we, as business owners and thought leaders, do more to reduce our footprint? How can we, as consumers, consume less?

Marit's tips to *Go Lightly*:

- Understand your power as a consumer: when you support a business with your dollars, you implicitly support their values and ethos.

- When you see something that's not right, speak your mind. The travel industry is entirely dependent on customer satisfaction, and businesses will adapt quickly when their bottom line is threatened.

- Ask to see the operator's sustainable tourism plan. How do they support the community, protect the environment they operate in, and address their carbon footprint?

The Camping Adventure

Nature is a potent salve for our souls. There really is nothing like stripping back to the bare essentials and reconnecting with the land to give yourself a sense of hope for the future. Listening to frogs croaking through tent walls, watching a sliver of silver moon slide behind the clouds, telling stories and drinking tea by an open fire and being woken naturally by the rising sun – this is how we find our way back home.

Heading out into the wild, we find a rest in the chaotic symphony of our lives, and allow our body clocks to reset so our balance with nature can be restored. It has been said that as citizens of the modern world we consume as much information each day as Shakespeare did over a lifetime, which is a terrifying thought. When we're living outside in nature, though, the mental whir we experience as a side effect of mental overconsumption slows dramatically. As our minds clear, we remember that we came from the Earth, and that we need to take care of it.

For those of us who dream of living digital-free or minimally, this is our chance to test that lifestyle, travelling with as little as possible. Camping gives us a taste of nomadic living, while allowing us to reclaim a large portion of our

travel budget. It also lets us tap into our spirit of adventure. Perhaps the most important thing we regain from a camping trip, however, is the ability to relinquish control. Things do go wrong when you're cooking your own food, sleeping in a tent and putting yourself at the mercy of the elements. But I couldn't imagine a more brilliant lesson in how we might all look at approaching life in a healthier way, welcoming whatever life throws at us with open hearts and minds.

Plan + Eco-Charge Your Camping Adventure

Setting

For the most remote locations, opt for backcountry camping in national parks, where you usually hike in and BYO water and food. For something more accessible, choose 'car camping' where you drive up to the site – you won't have to fully unpack, and these sites usually have bathrooms and maybe a little shop. If you don't want to compromise on style, glamping companies offer fully set-up camps with bell tents, queen-size beds and showers. Oh, and watch for the forest micro-hotels popping up around the world, by companies such as unyoked.co in Australia, and vipp.com in Europe.

Leave Only Footprints

Take your rubbish with you, and use chemical-free soaps, shampoos and sunscreens (see page 140) that won't damage soil or water, and biodegradable soap for your dishes, which should be washed 100 metres (330 feet) from the water source. Resist the urge to pick flowers or plants or disturb or feed wildlife, and prioritize camping spots with naturally cleared floors. Making a fire? Check they're permitted, BYO wood, only use well-established fire rings, keep them small and make sure they're completely extinguished. Even doing only one of these things would be hugely beneficial.

Activities

Think hiking, stargazing and foraging, al fresco yoga, swimming and birdwatching, with day trips into nearby towns to seek out small art galleries, organic cafés and live music. With kids? Throw scavenger hunts, card games and fishing into the mix.

Packing

Consider what's really going to make your trip enjoyable, then ditch everything else. If you're camping far from home or aren't sure you're going to camp again, rent or borrow gear including tents, inflatable mattresses and sleeping bags. If you do buy, prioritize pre-loved gear, or sustainable businesses such as nemoequipment.com or patagonia.com. A trowel is useful for DIY bathrooms (do your business 60 metres [200 feet] from a water source), as are solar lamps for evenings. Bring biodegradable rubbish bags to sort plastics, papers, cans and bottles for recycling once you leave and a mason jar for food scraps, which can be composted later.

Food

Wrap pre-prepared meals (in beeswax wraps, if you want to be nerdy), things like root vegetables and line-caught fish, storing in a cooler box then cooking them over the fire or camp stove. Cooked stews and curries are also great – you can freeze, use to keep your cooler cold, then eat as they defrost. Plan meals in advance to avoid waste, think minimal packaging, and avoid disposables by packing enamel, second-hand plastic or reusable bamboo crockery (sold in most camping stores). For water, bring reusable tanks.

Eat
Lightly

Our holiday 'foodprint' is just as important to consider as our transport emissions and accommodation impacts. If we all went vegan, we could cut our carbon emissions in half, but for those of us who can't or aren't ready to do that, or just want to know what else we can do, read on. Here we'll talk about choosing eateries that favour SLO (seasonal, local, organic) food, how mimicking locals often leads to better food choices, why we might avoid hotel buffets, which questions we can ask restaurateurs, and more.

Support Conscious Cafés

Every time we buy something to eat while we're travelling, we're voting with our dollars. So if you want to vote for keeping the places you love as healthy as they are unique, here are some things to put your money behind.

- Eateries that are locally owned and staffed so your money is going directly into the local economy. Generally these restaurants will be further away from the major tourist sites and won't have touts out front.

- Venues with their own vegetable gardens; and in developing nations, those that support local farmers with things like microloans and training.

- Eating home-cooked meals through apps such as EatWith, which links travellers to locals who want to cook for them in more than 130 countries.

- Menus filled with local ingredients, even if they terrify you. Food is a gateway to cultural understanding.

- Anything *without* palm oil in it; palm oil plantations are leading to deforestation across the globe.

- A third of the Earth's fresh water supply is used by the meat and dairy industry. Support vegan restaurants and hotels, or eat one more meat-free meal per week,

eat meat only once per week or month, or go vegan. Eating plant-based on the road is often the safest, cheapest and healthiest option, too.

If you're not an adventurous eater and prefer to stick to international chains, consider that they're often no faster or cheaper than local options.

Ask Good Questions

- **Can I please have my drink without a straw?**

- **The salmon dish sounds delicious, are you able to tell me where it comes from? Is it farmed or wild caught?**

- **Can you please tell me about local producers you use?**

- **Do you change your menu seasonally?**

- **Do you have any organic wines on your list?**

- **Have you ever considered using compostable packaging?**

Asking these kinds of questions (and learning how to ask them in the local language if you're travelling to a foreign country) might make you feel like a jerk, but they are necessary. You need to know the provenance and ethics surrounding what you're putting in your mouth if you want to make a difference, and no matter what the answer to these queries is, just asking them – in as polite and non-judgmental a way as possible – could change the model of the eatery you're in.

If enough people start asking for an alternative to plastic cups, or turning down meat that has been shipped all

Go Lightly Challenge

Think about a holiday you already have planned or one you're hoping to take in the near future. Choose ONE small thing you can do to reduce your negative impacts – always asking not to have a straw in your drink, for example – and make it your mission to ask about it in every eatery you enter. You can add on from there.

the way from the US in Australian restaurants, for example, the owners of these establishments will know these issues are important and will be compelled to make positive changes.

Mimic Locals

Whether it's deciding what to do, how to act or where to stay, shop or eat, behaving like a local leads to more sustainable travels across the board, more motivation to get out of the tourist bubble. In terms of food, it helps you avoid tourist trap restaurants, where locals would never usually dream of going.

I try never to leave a country without eating with a local. If this isn't possible, try asking residents where to find the hidden food gems and of-the-moment hotspots. Restaurant reviews in local papers are another great source of inspiration, since they won't be covering tourist traps (use Google Translate if you're in a foreign country). You can also head to food markets, asking stallholders about their favourite way to cook what you're buying, or enrol in a local cooking class.

Here's a radical idea: why not join the increasing number of travellers turning to food foraging as a way to experience destinations, and to connect to the natural world and their plates in a different way? An important skill to learn in an age of panic buying, and the number of guided foraging adventures in both urban and wild environments is growing.

Ditch the Buffet

With their bountiful baskets of fresh-baked goods, colourful fruit platters and bowls filled with steaming mushrooms and baked beans, hotel buffets are incredibly tempting, but also incredibly wasteful. Hotels want their breakfast buffets to look abundant, and they're terrified of upsetting guests thrilled by the idea of all-you-can-eat, leading to massive amounts of food getting binned every day at hotels all around the world.

The *New York Times* recently reported that the US generates 63 million tons of food waste every year, an estimated 40 per cent of which comes from consumer-serving businesses like hotels and restaurants.

Low-waste initiatives are being implemented by some big hotel chains, but in the meantime order à la carte instead, or eat at a locally owned café, letting the hotel owners know why you've decided to do that.

If you can't resist the buffet, consider how hungry you really are before stacking everything on your plate and tossing the remainder away. Businesses follow where consumers lead, so express your concern and ask hotel staff what they do with the waste from the buffet. And bring your reusable container to stock up on snacks for the day, since it's probably going to go to waste otherwise.

 ONE SMALL THING • If you want to minimize food waste further, consider sharing meals, requesting half-portions at restaurants, and bringing your reusable container to every meal so you can take leftovers away.

Rob Greenfield

Adventurer and activist, on mission-based travel **robgreenfield.org • @robjgreenfield**

'We can look at each trip as a sustainability mission, to make the world a better place.'

A self-described 'dude making a difference', Rob Greenfield has eaten from hundreds of dumpsters to oppose food waste, cycled across the US three times on a bamboo bicycle to spread his message of sustainability, worn a suit made from the trash created by the average American around the streets of New York for one month, grown and foraged 100 per cent of his food in 2018… the list goes on. Why does he do this? To inspire us all to live in a more regenerative way.

What does sustainable travel mean to you?
A better phrase is 'less destructive travel'. If the trip is by flight it's not sustainable; if it's by a fossil fuel-powered vehicle, like a car, it's not either. Even trains are just far *less* destructive. Truly sustainable travel would be a long hike, or a cycling or sailing trip.

Another example of 'real' sustainable travel?
Travel that doesn't just destroy less, but that also improves the place you visit. Staying, for example, on a regenerative agriculture farm where your money goes to supporting them and the local environment. Another great

example is WWOOFing (wwoof.net), where your travel makes you a better person by teaching you a skill.

Another pillar of your personal travel philosophy?

I don't stay in hotels, especially not for single nights. They're going to thoroughly clean it, using lots of water and electricity, they're going to wash the sheets after one use, I could go on. Instead, I stay with a local host or a friend whenever I can, and live like I would at home.

Your favourite green journey?

Last year I stayed at St Michael's Sustainable Community in Costa Rica. The house was built out of 95 per cent second-hand materials, all the greywater stayed on-site and watered food plants, and it was surrounded by a food forest. If you go to places that make you more environmentally conscious at home, then we're talking about sustainable travel because it's travel that has changed the course of your life.

The biggest mistake you've made in terms of sustainable travel?

Plenty of times I've eaten things I wouldn't at home because I couldn't find a better option, so planning ahead is really important. It's important to stay somewhere you can cook, rather than having to eat every meal out.

Rob's tips to *Go Lightly*:

- Lodge with locals, and think about it as if you're living with them, not just staying with them.

- Base your trip around hiking, biking or sailing.

- Carry a water purifier so you never need to buy bottled water.

The Road Trip

Long, empty highways, crumpled maps spread across the dashboard, hair whipping in the wind – there's a delicious sense of freedom woven into the fabric of road trips. They're deeply nostalgic, transporting us back to simpler times when air travel wasn't quite so cheap, when holidays were slower and when everyone just seemed to have more time.

When we travel by road we experience a deeper sense of place since we're immersed in the landscape. One of my favourite travel assignments was a road trip through northern Namibia and I'll never forget watching, as my local guide and I drove away from the Hoanib Valley, shale mountains give way to hills carpeted with soft grasses, then to swelling sand dunes as we approached the Skeleton Coast with its whale bones and shipwrecks. The journey was moody and atmospheric, and far more intriguing than any film I'd seen.

Easing into landscapes by road, rather than parachuting into them by air, gives our minds time to catch up to our bodies and to appreciate the places we see. Without a tight schedule, we road trippers are free to explore at our own pace and leave plenty of room for serendipity, and for chance encounters along the way.

Road trips are often accompanied by enchantingly long, rambling conversations with our travel companions, ones that are otherwise difficult to come by in our fast-paced lives. But equally enchanting are those lengthy stretches of silence, where we let our minds expand as the landscape slides by.

The best aspect of road trips, though, is that they're an instant escape hatch. When the weight of the world becomes too much, we can simply jump behind the wheel and take off, embracing all the unexpected detours along the way. Which, actually, just might be the perfect blueprint for approaching life once we return home.

Plan + Eco-Charge Your Road Trip

Route

Relish the journey, don't set yourself up for exhaustion. Choose your destination, divide the total distance by how much time you have, and try not to cram too much in. Three hours' driving each day would be ideal, as would taking the shortest route to reduce fuel consumption. Road trip apps such as Waze and Roadtrippers are helpful.

Stopping

Pick one or two must-sees each day, looking for less crowded spots that you'll likely have all to yourself. Following your own interests – whether that be music, literature, history or hiking – is always better than chasing busy attractions.

Packing

The lighter you pack, the less fuel you'll use and the more relaxed you'll be, not having to pull countless bags out of the car each night. Pack your reusable cup and bottle to avoid single-use plastics en route, and instead of wet wipes, pack a washcloth for refreshing.

Sharing

If your back seat is empty, consider signing up to sites like liftshare.com or blablacar.com and safely sharing your ride. This minimizes the number of cars on the road, and might introduce you to a fascinating new travel mate.

Entertainment

Download local music and podcasts about the region you're travelling in, to immerse yourself in the culture as you go. Pack a small portable speaker in case there isn't a Bluetooth-enabled sound system in the car.

Accommodation

Spontaneity is the lifeblood of road trips, but if you don't plan you'll likely have to compromise on more sustainable accommodation options. Pre-book great campsites, locally owned motels and B&Bs that reflect local flavour.

Food

Research where to get local, organic food en route, to avoid eating at fast-food chains. Look for fresh food markets, stocking up on picnic food with minimal packaging. If you're leaving from home, take road trip-friendly snacks like popcorn, bliss balls and trail mix in reusable containers.

Extras

If you can hire an electric vehicle for the journey, do it, or try for a hybrid or more fuel-efficient car. If there's cruise control, use it for more fuel efficiency. Also, turn off your engine whenever you stop for longer than a minute.

Travel Lightly

Leaving space and time for still-ness and reflection, and properly disconnecting from life back home so you can really sink into the destination, is vitally important in our fast-paced, instant gratification-filled world. In this section, we'll consider mindfulness practices to help you slow down and create more space in your travel days, look at the magic of leaving days free to do nothing at all, see if we can develop healthier behaviours around social media, and more.

Pack a Journal

An excellent tool for reflection, a journal has the added benefit of leaving you with a physical record of your travels. I've been a journaller since I was a kid and have a big box full – if my house caught fire, they'd be the first thing I'd take.

Whether you spend five minutes or an hour each day doing this, it makes you a more engaged traveller, and helps you purge your emotions and frustrations (I think of my journal as a free therapist) so you can stay focused as you explore. This isn't just about keeping notes about what you did each day. It's also about figuring out what your journeys mean to you.

Journalling Prompts

- **The strangest thing I saw today was...**

- **One cultural difference I noticed today was...**

- **The most awe-inspiring thing this week was...**

- **The biggest lesson I learned today was...**

- **Sit for ten minutes, whether you're in a jungle or a busy café. Observe what happens around you, then write about it, using your notebook like a camera.**

- **If you're using a journey to discover how to improve your life back home, try writing your own eulogy. Sounds mad, but diving into what made you of service to the world will help you envision how you can become that person. Trust me, it works.**

- **If writing isn't your thing, try sketching instead.**

Go Slow

What we're aiming for is the antithesis of fly-by tourism. Eschewing the five-cities-in-ten-days and three-churches-in-24-hours kind of travel, in favour of taking fewer but longer trips, and leaving time and space for lingering in cafés and people-watching. For long walks in nature, and even longer conversations with strangers. For avoiding the crowded tourist sites and discovering the appeal of doing 'normal' things in a place while living as a local.

Slowing down is essential to more sustainable travel. It reduces clogging of sections of a town or city and helps you understand the soul of a place. Travel is not a race, so let's try to do less. To let go of any FOMO (fear of missing out) we might attach to ticking off big-ticket sites, and instead spend at least some of our travel days giving our best imitation of a *flâneur* (or *flâneuse*), a French word for someone strolling a city's streets without any specific purpose except for capturing its essence. We'll discover things other travellers haven't, while gaining a deeper understanding of the everyday life of locals and likely growing more as people, too.

Five Slow-Living Resources

- *Slow Travel* (2019) by Penny Watson

- *Chasing Slow* (2017) by Erin Loechner

- *The Miracle of Mindfulness* (1975) by Thich Nhat Hanh

- The Slow Home podcast

- Sloww.co website

Photograph Mindfully

A woman stands on the ice in Antarctica in front of skyscraper-sized icebergs and thousands of penguins, but she's missing most of it. She has her phone up against the scene, documenting it but not really seeing any of it. I can judge that woman, because that woman was me. And while I like to say that constant documentation is an occupational hazard, the fact is I've missed dozens of once-in-a-lifetime travel moments by having my head buried in my camera.

When we're busy taking endless snaps, we're often missing other details that really bring a place to life, like the accents around us, or the smell of the food being cooked next to us, and are never fully surrendered to the experience. Having said that, taking photographs mindfully can help us slow down and carefully observe landscapes or people, enhancing our memories because of the concentration we're putting into the moment.

So let's take fewer and better-quality photographs, opting for real cameras over iPhones (an extra piece of luggage, but they help slow the speed of your photography down); make sure we're travelling for much more than just our Instagram feeds; and try to stay present as much as possible.

Go Lightly Challenge

Give yourself a quota of photos for the entire trip – one roll of film if you're going analogue, say, or one photo a day. You'll be forced to think deeply about each shot and why it's important, and will come home with a curated selection of really meaningful shots.

Share Consciously

It's easy to focus on the negative effects Instagram can have on travel, but search #sustainabletravel on Instagram and you'll find hundreds of thousands of people using it to highlight what's being done *right* – the excellent eco hotels and restaurants, the beach clean-ups, the cross-cultural connections and more.

If you are sharing a photo on social media, do it mindfully, asking yourself before posting:

- **Will this photo inspire my followers to make better choices when they travel?**

- **How could I caption this image to help my audience travel more lightly?**

- **Does this image reflect the reality of the situation?**

I ask myself these questions, and focus on sharing things such as campsites and hikes I discover, and thoughts around slow travel. I also show that I wear the same clothes many times. I urge you to do the same, and become part of the #proudtorewear movement.

In our increasingly filtered world, it's also more important than ever to be honest when we share. Cropping other tourists or rubbish out of a photo might make it look prettier but it can be misleading. Showing places just as they are, or writing about what you cropped out and why in the caption, will help your audience realize how overtouristed some places are, for example, helping them make better choices.

Jimmy Nelson

Photographer, on giving more than you take

@jimmy.nelson.official

'The real essence of wealth is giving more than you take.'

British photographer Jimmy Nelson is famous for his portraits of indigenous communities in some of the most isolated parts of the globe – Bhutan, Siberia, Papua New Guinea, Ethiopia and beyond. Published in his acclaimed book *Before They Pass Away* (2013), Nelson's work opens our eyes to the lessons we can learn from remote communities.

What does sustainable travel mean to you?

It means asking ourselves *why* we are taking each journey, and what we're giving back to the places and people we visit in return. It always has to be reciprocal.

What can we learn from meeting people so vastly different from ourselves when we travel?

That our unending need to consume, produce and purchase, and our idea that that will give us greater feelings of connection and value, is utterly wrong. We have everything we need. But we're locked into this economic spiral. Remote communities have something we don't: a deep connection to what it is to be human – physically, mentally, emotionally, culturally and animistically – and to the planet.

Your favourite green journey?

To the Marquesas Islands in the Pacific. When I first visited, I wanted to stay, but the locals said, 'We don't really want people like you,' then told me two stories. The first was about the French Post-Impressionist painter Paul Gauguin, who lived on the islands in the late 1800s and famously had sex with all the girls, and whom the locals loathed. The second story was about Jacques Brel, the French Elvis, and if I could emulate him I was welcome to stay. When Brel was diagnosed with terminal cancer in the 1970s, he took a journey of discovery, ending up on the Marquesas. The locals said, 'If you want to stay, you have to do something for us.' He went back to France, bought a biplane, and for the last 18 months of his life he was the islands' postman.

The biggest mistake you've made in terms of sustainable travel?

One day in Siberia, I was suffering in minus 50 degrees Celsius (minus 58 degrees Fahrenheit). I was told by locals to take all this synthetic clothing off and I was put in fur, and I've never been so warm in my life. I would never advocate wearing fur, but that situation taught me about listening to the communities I visit. This idea that we can buy comfort and safety – it's irrelevant.

Jimmy's tips to *Go Lightly*:

- Buy a second-hand analogue camera, and take a couple of rolls of film with you. The fewer images you take, the greater emotional investment you will put into them.

- Leave your smartphone behind, if you dare.

- Buy a paper map. This is how you find really off-track places, and it could be the key to avoiding overtourism.

The Retreat

It's no surprise that there has been a stratospheric rise in journeys designed specifically to bring more presence and clarity into our lives. Many of us are stuck behind computers for most of our waking hours, with our time dictated by an endless barrage of emails, messages and updates. To reward ourselves for all this hard work, we indulge in increasing amounts of consumption and distraction, which heaps more stress on to both ourselves and the Earth. No wonder we're all craving an escape from the virtual reality we inhabit.

Retreating allows us to return to a more essential human pace, so we can stop feeling overwhelmed, leaving room for compassion and understanding to slip through the door. It offers us the time and space we need to reprogramme our minds, which is exactly what we need if we're going to learn to treat our Earth with the love and respect it deserves.

Retreating doesn't necessarily mean splashing out on a fancy spa or yoga retreat, although it certainly can be that. It doesn't necessarily mean escaping to an ashram in India or a meditation retreat in Southeast Asia either, although it could be those things, too. All it really means is giving yourself an opportunity to rejuvenate your mind and body,

which could simply be heading to an eco cabin in the bush or a shack in a beach town near you. Anywhere you can switch off all your devices and reconnect with the natural world, your loved ones and, most importantly, yourself.

Whatever this journey ends up being for you, the key element is remaining fully present with everything you do when you're there – whether that be taking a photograph, eating a meal, showering or swimming in the ocean. By shutting out the digital world, recalibrating to the rhythms of the natural world and paying attention to each moment, we learn to properly appreciate the places we're in and become more mindful travellers. This, of course, has the side effect of compelling us to tread more lightly on the places we visit.

If switching off completely and surrendering to the natural world and your own naked mind terrifies you, remember that none of the urgent things we hurtle through our days doing could be more urgent than slowing down enough to enjoy our lives, rather than sleepwalking through them.

Plan + Eco-Charge Your Retreat

Digital Detox

Turn your email out-of-office responder on, block emails from being received (you can download plugins like Boomerang for this) and leave your laptop at home – your phone too, if you can manage it. It might feel as though you've had a limb removed at first, but it's important to wake up out of the digital trance. Take some reflective books instead. Three of my favourites include Zen master Thich Nhat Hanh's *Silence: The Power of Quiet in a World Full of Noise* (2015); Pulitzer Prize-winning poet Mary Oliver's nature-based poetry volume *A Thousand Mornings* (2012); and travel writer Pico Iyer's *The Art of Stillness* (2014).

Eating

According to Thich Nhat Hanh, everything we do, even banal everyday tasks like eating, can become a form of meditation. So let's give it a go. Whenever you eat on this trip, try to be fully present with your food. Think about all the elements – rain, sunshine, earth, air – and the work of the farmers and chefs that made the meal, mentally expressing gratitude for all their hard work. Be completely focused on the food as you eat, tuning into the tastes and textures, which makes it more enjoyable, and leaves you feeling satisfied after less. This is mindfulness 101, and can be extended to everything you do throughout your retreat.

Activities

Anything that leads to greater mind-clearing is welcome – meditation, yoga, massage, breath work. But really, the focus here is on being mindful with whatever you're doing, and on taking things as slowly as possible.

Accommodation

The more lo-fi, the better. Look for shacks, geodomes, retreats or cabins that are Wi-Fi- and TV-free or have no phone signal, ideally surrounded by nature so you can connect with the outdoors and your own creative energy.

Packing

Think things like hiking boots, swimming costumes and yoga mats that will inspire you to get outside and get moving, as well as notebooks, novels, sketch pads and analogue cameras. But this is really more about what you're *not* packing: leave your laptop, tablet and phone at home.

Impact
Lightly

Just witnessing the bad behaviour
we see while we're travelling –
from littering and wasting energy
and water, to trashy souvenirs and
environmental pollution – can be
anxiety-inducing. The best way to
avoid being overwhelmed and stay
positive? Be a living example of how
to do it right. In this section we'll
look at how to shop minimally and
mindfully for treasures, what it really
means to 'leave no trace', the power
of giving up geotagging, how to be
water wise, and more.

Leave No Trace

So simple, so brilliant. Leave the places you visit just as you found them, or better yet, improve them. Whether you're bouncing around a buzzy city or are in the middle of a remote forest, this means picking up your own trash, yes, but also the rubbish others have left on the beaches, city streets and hiking trails you come across as you travel. Remember the saying: 'We don't inherit the Earth from our ancestors, we borrow it from our children.'

If you're camping or hiking, 'leave no trace' extends to such things as leaving plants, rocks and other natural objects where you found them, not feeding wild animals, minimizing campfire impacts and making sure you dispose of your, umm, human waste in the right way (at least 60 metres [200 feet] from water, your camp and trails, in a 15 centimetre [6 inch] deep hole).

Clever companies such as take3.org and 10pieces.com.au encourage travellers to collect a few pieces of litter each day while they're travelling. Which sounds like a small thing… until you think about billions of people across the planet potentially doing it.

Go Lightly Challenge

Commit to picking up a certain amount of rubbish each day while you're away. Whether it's one, ten or 100 pieces, it will make a difference. Just make sure you're disposing of it in the right way (head to page 94 for tips) and have your tote bag with you always, so you can pop any trash you find into it as you go.

Shop Carefully

Step away from the cheap plastic tat and the internationally made luxury goods, and towards the locally made and hand-crafted. When you avoid mass-produced goods on your travels (which are often made in places far from where you are) you end up with more unusual souvenirs that you're likely to treasure forever, while supporting local artisans.

Mindful Shopping Tips

- Research where the best locally owned handicraft stores, markets, co-operatives or artisan workshops are.

- Look for well-crafted products made from natural materials that you'll actually use, for example handmade ceramics, textiles and baskets. Ask questions to make sure they really are handmade.

- Take it easy on the bargaining. It's always worth paying more for a carefully made product, and by investing in the work of artisans you're helping to keep artistic traditions alive.

- Visit artisan communities. You can meet the makers, learn about their craft and buy directly from them.

ONE SMALL THING • Often the gifts we buy our loved ones when we travel, no matter how well-intentioned or thoughtfully made, end up at the back of their cupboard or in the charity bin. Instead of physical gifts, try recreating a local meal you ate while you were away for them instead, sharing some local music, or simply sending them a handwritten postcard.

Avoid Geotagging

Increasingly, geotagged photos on social media giving exact location data are fuelling overtourism to once-pristine parts of the world. Just one of hundreds of recent examples is Delta Lake in Wyoming. The lake used to see one or two hikers a day, but after influencers with huge followings started posting photos there it received up to 145 people a day, leading to trail erosion and the draining of park resources.

Geotagging can also affect wild animal populations. On an assignment to Botswana, I was asked by guides not to geotag a photo I took of a group of rhinos, since poachers trawl the internet for exactly this kind of content.

Respect traditional landowners, too. In Australian Aboriginal law, for example, only certain people are allowed to visit some sacred landscapes. Take time to research the places you want to visit, to get properly informed about any pertinent ecological issues or indigenous beliefs. Consider:

- **Whose land am I on and is it appropriate for me to be here?**

- **What is the significance of this place?**

- **How do I move around in a respectful way?**

What to Do

Consider withholding location information when you share photos to help keep these places pristine, and avoid travelling just to get a certain Instagram shot. These days I never geotag my photos. Instead, let's seek out our own unique outdoor experiences where we can have a real connection to nature.

Be Water Wise

It's easy to become complacent about water at home – you turn the tap on, water comes out, you don't think too much about it. But it is estimated that by 2030 half the world's population will live in areas of water scarcity. Tourism unfortunately intensifies the problem, since hotel guests typically use more water than locals, so we need to do whatever we can to make sure local residents aren't being deprived of their essential supply because of us travellers.

How to Help

- Prioritize accommodations that use rainwater.

- Keep showers under three minutes. Wash your body and hair and save shaving legs for outside the shower.

- Pack darker clothes that need washing less often.

- Use your towels for as long as possible.

- Ask hotel management to install low-flow showers, and tell them about leaky taps or toilets.

- Visit everylastdrop.co.uk or wateruseitwisely.com for more ideas and information.

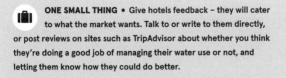 **ONE SMALL THING** • Give hotels feedback – they will cater to what the market wants. Talk to or write to them directly, or post reviews on sites such as TripAdvisor about whether you think they're doing a good job of managing their water use or not, and letting them know how they could do better.

Lisa Vitaris

Founder of 10 Pieces, on
reducing litter **10pieces.com.au**

'If everyone collects ten pieces of litter daily, that can make a huge difference.'

Having travelled to more than 100 countries and been exasperated by the amount of litter she found, in 2013 Australian Lisa Vitaris founded 10 Pieces, an initiative that works with more sustainable travel companies, asking travellers on their tours to collect ten pieces of litter as they go. Lisa's goal is to make litter collection a global movement and to help educate communities in such countries as Nepal, Bhutan, Peru and Tanzania about its benefits.

What does sustainable travel mean to you?

My sustainable travel mantra is 'take only photographs *and* ten pieces of litter, leave only footprints'. So taking out more litter than you take in, helping to make the world cleaner. It's amazing to see the effect on communities too. They think, 'Litter is obviously bad if people are coming to our country and picking it up, so maybe I won't do it.'

Is ten pieces really enough to make a difference?

The whole point of making it ten pieces is to make it really easy from the outset. It's about our collective power. So if you have ten people on a trip picking up ten pieces, that's

100 pieces; if you then get another group the next day that's another 100. That little effort can make a big difference.

Your favourite green journey?

To Socotra, a little island off Yemen, in 2019. I met a guy there who lives in a cave. The mouth of his cave is lined with oysters, there's a lagoon right out front which is home to turtles, mussels and scallops and other things he can eat, and he collects rainwater which he drinks and cooks with in tanks he pulled off a shipwreck. He took us walking across the lagoon and taught us about the different species in there, then we sat in his cave, he cooked us some scallops and we contemplated the world. Seeing the completely sustainable way he lived blew my mind.

The biggest mistake you've made in terms of sustainable travel?

I was in Bhutan doing the Jomolhari trek and there was heaps of litter up there – we picked up way more than ten pieces and brought it all back to camp. We were planning to safely incinerate it but then a local said, 'You can't incinerate because the mountain gods will be offended,' so we were stuck with it, at over 5,000 metres (16,400 feet). We ended up taking it out with us using our pack animals. That experience humbled me and made me realize you really need to work with locals to understand their perspective.

Lisa's tips to *Go Lightly*:

- Always take out more litter than you take in.

- Many people are paid to pick up litter, so make sure you're not doing someone out of a job by collecting it.

- Say no to single-use plastics.

The Boat Voyage

Considering that water is essential to our survival and the survival of the animals and plants we share our planet with, it's no wonder that so many of us feel so drawn to it when we travel. Being by the ocean reduces our anxiety, calms our nervous system and connects us to ourselves. Dive in and you can almost feel the water pulling the stress out of you. We feel very small in the ocean, a place where we're drawn away from our ego and where we can feel part of a much greater whole.

Boats give us entry to otherwise inaccessible coves and islands, making us feel more like explorers than tourists and filling us with a sense of freedom and adventure. Whether we opt for a chartered sailing trip, an electric- or solar-powered boat (yes, they exist) or even a kayak or canoe, travelling by water allows for a constant connection with nature, putting us just moments away from that endless, soothing expanse of blue. Falling asleep to the sound of lapping waves, waking to the rising sun throwing glitter across the water, knowing that there are wild creatures swimming all around us – it's all incredibly healing for our souls.

The more time we spend in the ocean, the greater sense of care we develop for it. At a time when carbon emissions are acidifying our waters, rising global temperatures are killing coral reefs, overfishing is devastating marine populations and at least 8 million tons of plastic is being dumped in our oceans each year, it's absolutely crucial that we nurture this sense of stewardship for our oceans. Mindful travel by water can be our gateway to all of this, and in turn helps us make better decisions when we're back on dry land.

Plan + Eco-Charge Your Boat Voyage

Choose Your Vessel

The lightest approach is kayaking or canoeing, but if you're after something less strenuous then charter a sailing boat, electric boat or solar-powered yacht – less harmful to marine environments than petrol-powered boats and quieter too (find these by typing 'electric boat hire in [your destination]' into your search engine). If you're not a sailor and don't fancy learning, hire a skipper, and maybe even a cook, with your boat. Sharing your trip with friends or other families will make this more cost-effective and less impactful, since it means fewer boats on the water, and much more fun.

Destinations

Instead of, say, joining a boat party in popular Croatia, Greece or French Polynesia, consider sailing around the islands and visiting under-touristed towns instead. Again, prioritize destinations closer to home, and those that aren't on the tourist trail.

Last Resort

If a motorboat is your only option, remember that gas and oil are extremely dangerous for aquatic environments, and keep an eye out for any fuel leaking into the water. Choose smaller and more lightweight boats, favouring light metals such as aluminium, since they're going to require less fuel. Many cruise liners have a higher environmental impact than planes, owing to their incredibly high fuel and electricity consumption, so consider letting them be the last option.

Packing

If you're planning on snorkelling or fishing, try to rent or borrow the gear, or buy pre-loved. Remember to pack light – you probably don't need the new swimsuit you have your eye on, or that plastic floating swan, but little extras like card games and books are a good idea. If whale- or dolphin-watching is on the agenda, bring binoculars.

Go Chemical-Free

When choosing a boat to hire, ask what the boat is painted with, making sure it's non-polluting. In the 1980s and '90s, the use of poison-laden antifouling paints was widespread; the aim was to kill barnacles on hulls, but many other sea creatures were poisoned in the process. Whether it's you or a company running the show, check how both blackwater (human waste) and greywater (untreated water coming from showers, sinks, dishwashers and washing machines, which often contains chemicals) are going to be dealt with during your time on board. Prioritize chemical-free body and hair wash, sunscreens labelled 'reef safe' and natural cleaning products, and minimize rubbish, making sure every piece stays on board until you're back on dry land.

Wild Lightly

When done right, wildlife tourism helps us appreciate and support animals and their environments, but when it's not it can be a nasty, abusive business with horrific consequences. In the following pages, we'll look at what we can do to prioritize animal welfare, including how to safari smartly, what to avoid when it comes to zoos, aquariums and animal rehabilitation centres, why it's important to avoid animal artefacts, why we should focus on wildlife holidays that contribute to the conservation of animals and their habitats, and more.

Respect Animals

I have ridden an elephant. I'm ashamed to admit it, but I did it in Nepal seven years ago. The experience made me realize that the tourism industry too often exploits animals, and that we can become part of that abuse without even realizing it. According to World Animal Protection, more than 550,000 animals suffer every day from tourist operations and attractions, but most visitors are unaware that the animals have often been abused, 'broken in' or drugged to ensure they give rides and perform tricks. Luckily, the more informed we are, the better choices we can make. If you are planning on visiting a wildlife tourist attraction and aren't sure about whether it's humane, ask yourself:

- **Are these animals behaving completely naturally, just as they would in the wild?**

- **Are they being exploited in any way for my enjoyment?**

- **Why am I so desperate to see this animal up close?**

- **Is there a way I can see them in their natural habitat instead?**

How to Help

Whether it's riding camels in India or cuddling baby tigers in Thailand, any situation where an animal is forced to behave in opposition to their natural instincts should be avoided. The truth is, any animal that's in a captive situation – be it a zoo, circus or aquarium – is not behaving as it would in the wild. Other situations to be wary of include:

- Shark diving, where sharks are attracted by buckets of entrails, which disrupts their natural behaviour and feeding patterns.

- Rodeos or bullfights.

- Visiting dolphins and whales in marine parks, where their life expectancy is only half that of a wild dolphin or whale.

- Cuddling animals inside zoos and sanctuaries. If they are operating ethically, they shouldn't be offering close contact with animals.

- If you see captive animals being exploited, report it to bornfree.org.uk.

One of the best ways we can end animal abuse in the travel industry is to vote with our dollars, and stop attending harmful attractions. Even rehabilitation centres need to be regarded with scepticism, since many can be captive wildlife viewing centres in disguise.

If you love animals and want to ensure their health and happiness, stick to observing them in the wild, from a distance. A great rule generally when it comes to sustainable travel is to always leave things in as natural a state as possible.

Refuse Animal Artefacts

The best way to do no harm is to avoid artefacts made from animal materials at all costs. But just so we know why, here's a little background on some of the biggest issues related to these products.

In most countries, 'tortoiseshell' is now made of plastic, but in Central America and Southeast Asia many souvenirs are still made of the shell of the endangered hawksbill sea turtle. If you want to help save the hawksbill, ask the seller what the product is made of. If they say tortoiseshell, let them know why you don't want to buy it (sellers themselves might not know it's a problem) and ask if they have something not made from animal products to let them know that's your preference.

With the warming of our oceans and the deterioration of many coral reefs, we need to treat coral like an endangered species and not buy it. Coral isn't actually a rock or a plant, but a colony of animals called polyps; it supports one quarter of other ocean animals and once harvested, it can take decades to grow back. Another obvious product to steer clear of is ivory, since the greatest threat to elephants is the ivory trade, with tens of thousands of elephants killed annually for their tusks. The trade in ivory is prohibited under international law.

Other Products to Avoid

- Feathers and furs.

- Snake wine (where snakes are infused in rice wine).

- Reptile-skin accessories.

- Traditional medicines that might contain exotic species.

- Wooden items, since certain woods are on endangered lists.

Safari Smartly

Taking a safari where you can observe animals in their natural habitat is one of the most ethical ways to interact with animals on your travels, especially since visiting the national parks they're conducted in can help with wildlife conservation. During COVID, poaching levels escalated due to national park workers being laid off and fewer tourists (tourists offer indirect protection – more eyes and ears). The lack of tourist dollars saw many conservation projects fall over, particularly in Africa. Some factors to consider to ensure you're doing the best thing by the animals you're there to see:

- Investigate which safari destinations are the most sustainable – where tourism, community and conservation are interconnected. Rwanda, Botswana and Namibia in Africa, or Tortuguero in Costa Rica, have great track records.

- Give preference to operators with a commitment to conservation and sustainability or regeneration – wilderness-safaris.com, for example, is excellent.

- Consider rewilding or citizen science trips, where you get involved in projects that repair environmental damage and bolster populations of endangered species, often alongside local scientists and researchers. See rewildingeurope.com or biosphere-expeditions.org for more info.

- If you're with a guide, listen to them when they tell you to stay in the vehicle, keep quiet or ask you not to share photographs of endangered species.

- Avoid putting pressure on guides to 'tick off' animals you want to see, which could push them into bad behaviour in pursuit of tips.

- If you're doing a self-drive safari, stick to the designated roads, give wildlife plenty of space so as not to impact their natural behaviour too much, and never get between adults and their young.

Go Lightly Challenge

Spend a full day wildlife watching without your drone, phone or camera. Instead, take your journal or notepad and, after observing the animal for a chunk of time, try drawing it. It doesn't matter how artistic you are – it's the act that counts, and the deep concentration it requires.

During a road trip through Namibia in 2019, I learned how this southern African nation, realizing the vital role wildlife and landscapes played in attracting tourism, was the first African country to write provisions for environmental protection and conservation of natural resources into its constitution. Community conservancies and privately owned reserves now cover about a sixth of the country's land mass, and many of these host eco lodges that are majority owned and run by locals, funnelling money back into local communities. This trip opened my eyes to how tourism could be used in a more symbiotic way, and to how important it is to put destinations that need tourism to protect species and environments, first.

Drone Wisely

It might seem harmless enough, flying a small drone over animals to photograph them in their habitat, but drones can stress wildlife. A viral 2018 video posted on *National Geographic*'s website highlighted this really well – it showed a brown bear mother and cub in Russia, with the cub repeatedly falling down a treacherous, snow-covered slope because of a drone being flown overhead. Check it out for proof of how traumatic these machines can be for animals.

The noise and visual presence of drones can cause animals to experience increased heart rate, stress that could end up disrupting their reproductive process, and other stress responses like running or flying away, or avoiding areas where drones are frequently used, which could end up affecting a whole population.

As drones become smaller and cheaper and more of us have them, we should try to help minimize their impact on wildlife. Before pulling your drone out, consider *why* you want to take the video and whether you really need to. If it's for scientific studies or a conservation project, that's one thing, but stressing an animal out or even risking its life to make an impact online is not OK.

Beks Ndlovu

Founder of African Bush Camps,
on supporting local communities

africanbushcamps.com • @africanbushcamps

'Travel is nurturing for us travellers.
We have a responsibility to ensure the
communities and environments we visit
receive that nourishment too.'

In 2006, Zimbabwean Beks Ndlovu founded African Bush
Camps, which has 15 luxury tented bush camps and lodges
in Botswana, Zambia and Zimbabwe. He is one of a
handful of black CEOs in the African safari industry.
Ndlovu places sustainable tourism at the heart of his
company, prioritizing meaningful interactions with,
and contributions to, local communities and wildlife.

What does sustainable travel mean to you?
So many of us separate ourselves from nature. Once we
know how interdependent we are, we can begin to understand
the responsibility we have to feed the environments and
communities we visit, in the same way they feed us.

**Is more diversity in the safari industry, including in senior positions,
part of moving towards a more sustainable travel future?**
My ability to have impact and get the attention of the local
communities I work with has come from earning respect over
time. I am from these communities, I am one of them. The more
we can create ambassadors from these local communities, who
are passionate about where they come from, the easier our

conservation efforts will be and the more wins we enjoy. It's
also critical for us to attract more travellers of colour.

Your favourite green journey?

A ten-day expedition in the Congo in February 2020, through
savannahs and forests. We spent a lot of time on foot, and
stayed in humble camps that allowed us to connect with local
people like the Ba'Aka pygmy tribe. We saw how the Ba'Aka
hunt with handmade nets in the forest, and how they sing and
chant, commune and share, as most of us did hundreds of years
ago. Witnessing these ancient ways reminded me about the
importance of learning to collaborate, especially now.

The biggest mistake you've made in terms of sustainable travel?

Travelling to cover as much ground as possible, in the US
in 2003. The trip was exhausting, and it reminded me of the
importance of travellers leaving time to immerse themselves
in experiences. Movement doesn't necessarily equate to
satisfaction or a better understanding of an area.

What is your utopian vision of the future of travel?

For travel, especially travel linked to conservation, to
be viewed as integral to livelihoods. Until that happens,
governments won't take it as seriously as they should.

Beks' tips to *Go Lightly*:

- Do your research. Choose accommodations that are eco-
  friendly and that support locals.

- Take the most sustainable transport to your destination.

- Understand that sometimes you might pay a higher price for
  experiences with less impact, but it will be worth it.

The Wildlife Safari

Observing animals in their natural habitat can be a powerful way of helping us fall deeper in love with the natural world, while also teaching us important life lessons. Whether we're watching elephants and zebras on an African safari, spotting orcas around the UK or finding sloths in the Costa Rican jungle, the more time we spend observing animals, the greater connection and respect we feel towards them.

Watching the tight community dynamics of animals play out in the natural world can be a potent reminder of the interconnectedness of all things. It can also teach us about collaborating, learning to relax and the importance of play.

Reconnecting with nature is also a form of spiritual renewal, one that's particularly needed in our materialistic, industrialized society. The future of humanity will depend, increasingly, on the realization that the Earth isn't just a place we inhabit, but that we *are* the Earth – and that if the Earth is not doing well, we are not doing well.

Realizing the vital role wildlife and landscapes play in attracting tourism, many nations around the world have taken measures to conserve and protect them, so by travelling with wildlife front of mind we can really put our tourism dollars

to good use. If done the right way, tourism can help wildlife populations grow, protect landscapes and unique ecosystems, increase the incomes and quality of life of locals, and improve the economic outlook for entire countries.

When we see animals in the wild, we also become ambassadors for them. I'll never forget observing polar bears during a travel writing assignment in the Canadian Arctic. The melting of the Arctic ice means their seal hunting season is shorter, which ultimately leads to a declining population. The polar bears have no way of protecting themselves from this – only our actions will have an effect. The idea for this book surfaced shortly after that awakening experience.

Plan + Eco-Charge Your Wildlife Safari

Choose Your Destination

Prioritize those that put conservation first – ones that use ecotourism to enhance education and financially benefit local people, protect wildlife and landscapes and offer green accommodation and food options. Also give under-touristed destinations preference, consciously choosing destinations that need support.

Soften Your Footprint

Consider multi-day walking safaris – they're much more peaceful and liberating, and let you see and hear nature in ways you don't from a vehicle. Imagine putting your hand inside an elephant's dusty footprint or touching the rough trunk of an acacia tree, nothing but the crunch of your boots and the sharp trill of birdsong as your soundtrack. If you're opting to self-drive, make sure to stick to the designated roads. Eliminate internal flights wherever possible, and opt for either wild camping, eco lodges or demountable camps.

Research

The more research you do about the wildlife, landscapes and cultures you'll encounter, the better questions you'll have for your guides, and the greater respect you'll develop for the destination. Especially important if you have kids, since you can pass that information on to them.

Packing

Think earth-toned clothing that blends into the environment in lightweight fabrics. Pack a hat, a bandana to douse in water and wrap around your neck when it's hot, a beanie, gloves and sweater for dawn and dusk (animals are most active during these times, so most safari-style experiences happen then) and lightweight walking shoes with good tread. Pack light to stay nimble while journeying through rough terrain – a lightweight duffel bag without wheels is ideal, plus a small backpack for day trips. If you're into photography, a good zoom lens is recommended (try buying second-hand). Sites like borrowlenses.com also let you rent camera gear.

Avoid Disappointment

This is the wild, not a zoo, and there's no guarantee you'll see all the wildlife you'd like to. Avoid disappointment by paying attention to birds, smaller animals, insects, animal tracks and local flora too, opening up a whole new world.

View Animals Responsibly

Give animals space, don't use cameras or drones in a way that might scare them, keep your voice down and your phone on silent, and always listen to your guide. Most are highly trained, and are trying to keep both you and the animals safe.

Connect
Lightly

Connecting with other human beings is, for many of us, the reason we travel. We want to see how other cultures live, understand how they differ from and are similar to us, and return home filled with ideas for how we might live our lives better. Connecting with other cultures reminds us that we're all part of the same human tribe – which is more essential today than ever. Here, we'll look at how we can ensure we're respecting all lives as much as we do those of our family and friends back home, the best ways to give back to communities in need, why it's important to choose local guides, and more.

Respect All Cultures

I think of visiting another country as being invited inside someone else's home. The inhabitants have opened the door very wide for us to be there, so we want to be good guests. This is all about good manners – being polite, gracious and a good ambassador for your country.

If you want to photograph someone, ask them or gesture to your camera if you don't speak the language. If they say yes, offer to show them the photo on the screen or to send it to them, to foster a deeper connection. We've become too accustomed to using the world's inhabitants as our Instagram backdrop, which can lead to shallow depictions of cultures.

I have definitely been guilty of this. Travelling in Ethiopia's Omo Valley a few years ago, my husband and I visited a village where we were encouraged to pay members of the tribe to let us take photos of them. And while there was reciprocity – the tribespeople were earning an income from us – it was far from an authentic experience and felt almost as though we were visiting a human zoo.

Let's put our cameras down and start conversations instead. Hopefully, this increased openness will make us better able to embrace diversity when we arrive home, too.

How to Be a Good Guest

- If you want to talk to someone, try to speak a few words of their language.

- If someone doesn't want to be photographed, or if you're unsure of consent, respect that and move on.

- Approach locals politely. Smile, ask questions, thank them. First-hand experience helps us resist stereotyping.

Give Well

When we're travelling to countries less fortunate than our own, we instinctually want to help. It takes a hard heart to feel nothing when a child beggar knocks on our taxi window, but in many countries, criminal gangs run these begging rackets. Give to the beggar, and you are bolstering the power of those gangs and locking the kids into a cycle of poverty.

Instead, give to reputable charities, which have spent huge amounts of time and resources investigating how to best tackle the issue (I find charitynavigator.org useful for finding trustworthy charities). If you want to give directly, carry some fruit or other healthy food with you in your tote bag.

If you've connected with a particular community – perhaps you've been staying in a small village or a homestay – that you want to help, ask politely if there's any way you could do that. This might be looking after their kids for a day, fixing something around their house, helping out with their farming for a day, or doing the grocery run.

You can also choose to travel with a company that focuses on social justice. Justice.travel, for example, brings travel and human rights together through its trips to Colombia, Mexico and Guatemala, where travellers learn about local issues from activists and journalists, then return home as knowledgeable advocates.

ONE SMALL THING • Slum tourism is a growing trend. More than a million tourists a year visit slums in such cities as Rio de Janeiro, Johannesburg and Mumbai, but the phenomenon has been accused by some as being voyeuristic. Before booking a slum tour, question why you want to take it, and ask operators how much of the money you spend doing it goes back into the community.

Volunteer Right

'Voluntourism' has become a hot travel trend, one that is now reportedly worth US $1.7 billion worldwide, but it often does more harm than good. Purpose-hungry travellers who pay big money to volunteer somewhere, doing such things as building houses or schools, could be causing skilled locals to miss out on jobs because they're filling their positions.

Volunteer programmes and orphanage visits have also now been recognized as a major source of trafficking and exploitation. According to Save the Children, 8 million children worldwide are in orphanages, but up to 90 per cent of those aren't actually orphans – they are bought or leased from their parents, with operators simply trying to turn a profit.

Of course, it's a wonderful thing to want to make a difference and give back, and there are ways to volunteer responsibly and have a positive impact on the places you visit. By focusing on helping to train and empower local staff, you are passing on skills that they can then use within their community once you leave. Instead of volunteering at an orphanage, for example, consider supporting projects that help keep families together, such as income generation and social support programmes.

If you do want to take part in a regular volunteer programme, scrutinize operators about how much

ONE SMALL THING • One of the best ways to give back is by visiting devastated communities after natural disasters, since travel and tourism has proven to be one of the fastest routes to recovery in, for example, Puerto Rico after the 2017 hurricane, Sri Lanka after the 2019 terrorist attacks, and Australia after the 2020 bushfires. Well-managed tourism can be a lifeline for communities hit by the unexpected.

of your money stays in the community or charity. Speak with previous volunteers about their experience, and ask yourself: would I be comfortable with this situation at home?

Choose Local Guides

No matter how self-sufficient we might feel, there are always instances when we could use the help of a guide. Guides who have been born and raised in a place (or are at least long-term residents) know that place intimately, getting you to the most isolated hiking trails, introducing you to local tribes or taking you to those fabulous hole-in-the-wall restaurants.

They help you get to know the culture on a deeper level, giving you that vitally important local perspective and throwing light on key issues. Most importantly, employing local guides ensures that your tourism dollar goes directly into the community.

How Do You Find Good Local Guides?

- Ask friends and people you trust – personal recommendations are always best.

- Ask hotel staff. If they're on an ethical mission, they'll be able to point you in the direction of guides, restaurants and shops that are doing things in a more sustainable way.

- Try Airbnb Experiences for great citizen guides, and unique classes run by locals – from snow-hiking in Hokkaido to windsurfing in Sydney.

- Use websites such as cityunscripted.com, globalgreeternetwork.info, toursbylocals.com or viator.com to connect with small, independent companies on the ground or individual experts in thousands of destinations.

- Seek tour companies that use knowledgeable local guides – audleytravel.com, gadventures.com or muchbetteradventures.com are a few good examples.

Promote Porters' Rights

If you're hiking up mountains in Peru, Tanzania, Nepal or beyond, you'll likely want or need to hire a porter. But bear in mind that porters often endure terrible conditions, spend large chunks of time away from their families and, in places like Mount Everest, are often risking their lives. It's up to us to ensure they're being treated well and given the necessary support – the same support you or I might expect if we were doing their job.

Go Lightly Challenge

A positive headspace has been proven to activate our brain's prefrontal cortex, which leads to more creative thinking and better problem solving, something that's essential if we want to heal our planet. So grab some paper, and write or draw your utopian vision of the future of travel. Are there high-speed solar-powered rail networks criss-crossing the globe? Are single-use plastics banned worldwide? Does each traveller have to sign a sustainable travel pledge? Is one day of every week completely flight-free, worldwide? We can't create change if we can't envision it clearly first.

You can choose to travel with a company that promotes porter's rights, such as intrepidtravel.com or worldexpeditions.com. But you can also directly protect their rights by making sure porters:

- Have appropriate clothing for the season and altitude (proper footwear, wind- and waterproof clothing, sunglasses, hats).

- Are never asked to carry loads that are too heavy, usually below 30 kilos (66 pounds).

- Have a decent place to sleep each night.

- Are receiving a good working wage and three meals a day.

- Are over the age of 16 and below the age of 50.

If these things aren't in place ask your tour leader why, and let them know what needs to change. And give your porter as generous a tip as you can, never forgetting that you couldn't have had this extraordinary experience without them.

Caitlin Garcia-Ahern

Founder of Thread Caravan, on cultural conservation **threadcaravan.com • @threadcaravan**

'Preserving cultural traditions is important for the health of our planet.'

Through hosting week-long art workshops via her company Thread Caravan, Caitlin Garcia-Ahern connects travellers with local makers from indigenous communities. Whether she's escorting guests in her hometown of Oaxaca, Mexico, to dig clay to create ceramics or to Panama to stay on a sailboat while learning about indigenous embroidery, Garcia-Ahern is facilitating cross-cultural connections.

What does sustainable travel mean to you?
Leaving a place as we found it or better, and being really mindful about how we're interacting with local people and how we're affecting natural resources.

What does teaching cultural traditions bring to a traveller's life?
Obviously it connects people who enjoy handmade processes and artisan goods directly to the makers. But also, the indigenous communities we employ have been working in harmony with the land for thousands of years. In Guatemala for example, the weavers we employ for workshops use organic rather than GMO monocrop cotton, and natural dyes. Exposing travellers to that can really shift their mindset.

Your favourite green journey?

To Chambok in 2013, a small agricultural community in Cambodia. We stayed and ate in homestays, there were no hotels or restaurants, and we lived as our hosts did, taking bucket showers in the garden and hiking in the mountains. It was inspiring to see the low environmental impact, but high cultural benefits and the community income it generated.

The biggest mistake you've made in terms of sustainable travel?

When I was 18 I travelled to Guatemala and, with the best intentions, paid a lot of money as a volunteer to build a house. I've since learned that most volunteer home-building projects take down what you've built and reconstruct it using local workers. These days, I almost always advocate for not volunteering. We must ask locals what they need, rather than giving what we think is best.

How can travellers shop more sustainably in a destination?

Try to get as close to the maker as you can. Find shops that are co-operatively owned, or buy directly from studios. When you are buying something, make sure that it has some social impact, that it's well made, that you know where the resources come from, and that it's something you'll use.

Caitlin's tips to *Go Lightly*:

- When engaging with locals, particularly if you're learning from them, ask: what can I share in exchange?

- Research the resources of your destination, to make sure you're using them in the most sustainable way possible.

- Find a tour company or local guide that can open your mind, so you go home filled with questions.

The Learning Holiday

Vision and radical thinking are desperately needed in order to build a brighter future for our planet. So the more we can foster our creative imaginations while we travel, the better. Whether you're travelling to learn a language, a new style of cooking or farming, or art forms like ceramics, writing or photography, approaching travel this way can also transform it into a cultural narrative, one that allows you to experience a place through the stories of its artists and makers.

These immersive learning experiences require a more serious commitment from travellers, often forcing us to stay in one place for a period of time and to decelerate our pace while we're there, which is as good for the destination as it is for us. Learning holidays also often put us in direct contact with the indigenous communities we're learning from, who are also the custodians of traditional ecological knowledge.

Years ago I travelled to Mongolia on a photography workshop for a travel writing assignment. As well as vastly improving my skills, experiencing the local culture through the intimate lens of the camera also taught me about the rituals and etiquette that Mongolians' lives are steeped in, and details about their nomadic existence that made me

realize how little in life we need to be happy. Watching them take only what they needed from the Earth, and using it in a way that meant nothing went to waste, showed me that they saw themselves as just one species in this greater web of life.

Travelling to learn gives you skills for life, rendering you a more nuanced, imaginative version of yourself, and allowing you to pay it forward by teaching friends and family when you're back home. By learning skills from indigenous artisans, you're also participating in the fight to keep important cultural traditions alive, and are ensuring that the artisans teaching them can continue to generate an income from their craft. This is vitally important for safeguarding unique cultures around the world for future generations.

Plan + Eco-Charge Your Learning Holiday

Choose Your Style

Whether it's painting or pottery, dancing or poetry you want to learn, you'll need to choose whether to enlist the help of a company that specializes in creative and learning holidays, such as frui.co.uk, or whether to go it alone. Instead of going on a specific painting holiday, for example, you could simply choose the destination you'd like to visit, sign up to regular painting classes while you're there and practise on the other days while living life as a local. The more immersive, relaxed option if time is on your side.

Learn the Language

This is important for all travel, but since you're probably going to be interacting with locals more often during a learning holiday, put in extra effort. Study conversational phrases, as well as vocabulary specific to the skill you're learning, so you can get as much as possible out of the experience and share knowledge with your teachers, too.

Give More Than You Take

Whether you've financially compensated someone to teach you a skill or not, it's always important to ask what you can give in exchange for the skills you're learning. Maybe you have a unique skill of your own you can teach, maybe you can give language skills in return – whatever it is, always give as you take.

Pack a Notebook

A notebook (made from post-consumer recycled paper, of course) will be your best friend, whether it's permaculture, silversmithing or embroidery you're learning while you're away. Writing down what you learn by hand will not only solidify it in your brain and lead to richer memories of the experience, it will also give you a written record for when you're trying to recall it all later.

With Kids

Whether it's learning to surf, cook, paint, farm or horse ride, learning holidays are the best kind you can have with kids. They're engaged the whole time, they're learning alongside you which forges deeper bonds between you, and you're supporting their explorative urge as much as your own.

Bring it Home

Continue the learning process back home, attending courses and classes, both to deepen the knowledge and to share with others what you learned while you were away.

Return Lightly

Our journeys don't end when we come home and unpack our suitcases. In fact, that's when the real magic begins, when we let the places we visited burrow deep into our souls so we can continue to carry them around inside us. This is the time for sharing the road and all we learned along it with friends and family, for continuing the connections we made, for giving thanks to the businesses we encountered that did an exceptional job (and gentle hints to those that didn't), and for extending the impact of our journey for as long as possible.

Continue Connections

If we want to deepen and sustain our journeys, allowing them to continue to ripple through our lives once we're home, we can begin by continuing the connections we made while we were away – with both locals and other travellers.

Luckily, this is easier now than ever before. I have a continuing WhatsApp friendship with a guide I met during a recent trip to Mumbai, and with a host family I stayed with in Nepal years ago, and one of my best friends is a Dutch woman I met while staying in an ashram in India. This is how we can forge real, meaningful connections once our journeys are over, and how we can continue to learn first-hand about a country once we're no longer there.

Even better than jumping on email, text, social media or Skype, is handwriting your new friends a letter or postcard, maybe sparking an old-fashioned pen pal relationship. There's something especially potent about knowing that that piece of paper you're receiving has come from the country you loved, or has been touched by the hands of the person who made such an impression on you, and these letters can become much more meaningful than any souvenir.

Share Sustainably

We're all trying to do better, to be kinder to this one planet we have, and we're desperate for inspiration for how we can do that. Luckily, we live in a world where it's easier than ever to share with people from all over the world.

Use your social channels to share your conscious travel experiences, talking to your wider community about why you chose to travel to one place instead of five on your latest trip, why you picked a train over a plane, the amazing permaculture farm you stayed on, or all the weird and wonderful places your reusable cup ended up.

When you see your family and friends and they ask how your trip was, tell them about the excellent eco lodge you stayed in and why you chose it (without being preachy; no one likes that), or about the citizen science research you did during that epic hike. Hopefully they'll catch a little of your spirit and curiosity, and it might inspire them to seek something different on their next journey. When enough of us get talking about these things, gradually, we change the culture.

Five Illuminating Sustainability Documentaries

- *2040* (2019) – imagines solutions to climate change using existing technologies, on iTunes.

- *The True Cost* (2015) – examines the effects of fast fashion on people and the planet, on iTunes.

- *Virunga* (2014) – documents the fight to save mountain gorillas in the Congo, on netflix.com.

- *Gringo Trails* (2013) – covers overtourism, on vimeo.com.

- *Chasing Ice* (2012) – looks at climate change effects on our polar regions, on netflix.com.

Give Feedback

If we want to change outdated systems and behaviours in the travel world and create a better future, we need to speak up.

Pull out your laptop, and start sending emails. Emails of appreciation to all those excellent eco lodges, homestays, off-grid camps, local guides and sustainable travel companies you encountered who were doing things right and who deserve your support. Also the more difficult emails – to the hotels you believe were greenwashing, companies who weren't making an effort to minimize their footprint, or restaurants serving endangered species such as bluefin tuna (TripAdvisor reviews are great for this too). I often use the 'grace sandwich' method; give some praise first, sandwich the complaint in the middle, then end on another positive. By communicating your concerns, you're helping to hold these businesses accountable for their actions, and inspiring them to investigate more environmentally friendly options.

This kind of action takes effort, and courage, and it can feel futile. But disengaging or blinding ourselves to our moral responsibilities isn't an option any more. If we want our planet to survive, we have to make changes and inspire others to do the same. There is no more time to lose.

Live as a Traveller

Living at home as though on the road. What a magnificent concept. Once we've lived with less for a spell on the road, we often realize how much less we could be consuming at home. Since we've been trying hard to make the right choices each day when it comes to the way we stay, eat, drink and shop while we're away, we can try harder to make these same choices at home. Things like:

- Saying no to single-use plastics.

- Supporting locally owned businesses.

- Buying fewer (or no) new clothes.

- Keeping our spirit of curiosity and openness alive.

- Connecting with strangers in our own neighbourhoods.

- Exploring our own towns with the eyes of a traveller.

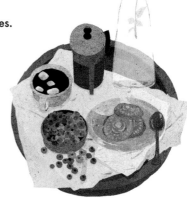

Let us not forget what we learned on our trails. Let us scoop up the most important learnings, press them close to our hearts, and promise ourselves to live at home as though on the road – lightly, curiously, and full of hope and wonder.

Four More Sustainability Books

- *The Future We Choose* (2020), by Christiana Figueres and Tom Rivett-Carnac.

- *The Uninhabitable Earth: A Story of the Future* (2019), by David Wallace-Wells.

- *Rise & Resist: How to Change the World* (2018), by Clare Press.

- *This Changes Everything: Capitalism vs. the Climate* (2014), by Naomi Klein.

Ben Bressler

Founder of Natural Habitat Adventures,
on making sustainable travel mainstream

nathab.com • @naturalhabitatadventures

'You emit greenhouse gases when you travel. Think about that, and only choose trips that are important to you.'

In 2007, Ben Bressler turned his company Natural Habitat Adventures into the world's first carbon neutral travel company, partnering with the non-profit Sustainable Travel International. Natural Habitat Adventures runs small group trips to wild areas in remote destinations, making sure money stays with local communities and that travellers tread as lightly as possible; it has a sustainability director, and in 2019 also ran the world's first zero-waste trip. Bressler's ambition is to use adventure travel to build support for the fight against climate change.

What does sustainable travel mean to you?

It means changing the way everyone thinks about travel, so that even the giant mass-tourism companies will start to look at sustainable travel and say, 'That's a valid segment, we want to get involved.' If a few small companies do it, it's nice, but meaningless for the planet. We all have to do it.

Your favourite green journey?

Going to see mountain gorillas in Rwanda. Travel can be bad for the environment. On the other hand, if it weren't for travellers those mountain gorillas wouldn't exist, and many species are in that same boat. The Virunga region, where the mountain gorillas live, would all be farmed if it weren't protected, and it's often habitat loss that causes species to disappear. The government of Rwanda recognizes that there's revenue to be made for the local people from tourists, so they protect the environment that draws them.

The biggest mistake you've made in terms of sustainable travel?
Many years ago, when we started doing trips to visit baby harp seals on the east coast of Canada to replace seal hunting with seal watching, I ended up getting punched in the face by a local seal hunter. I went there with the idea that these hunters were bad people, when in fact they were good people who needed an alternative way to make a living. I ended up becoming friends with that guy and some of the other hunters and we hired them as guides to take our guests out to see these baby seals, which they are now protecting.

The biggest change that needs to happen in travel?
Lowering carbon emissions is the biggest challenge we have. When people start demanding more sustainable travel options, and once there's money in it, the mega companies will get into it too. Oh, and electric planes would be fantastic.

Ben's tips to *Go Lightly*:

- Once you've taken a sustainably minded trip, tell others about it. We have to get this into the mainstream.

- Choose a company that shares your ethos on travel, because your guides and co-travellers will be focused on that.

- Offset your carbon emissions.

The Green City Break

Exploring another city is one of the best ways we can put a mirror up to our lives back home, introducing us to new ways of living while simultaneously infusing us with high doses of culture, architecture and history. But if we want to make sure we're doing this in the most sustainable way possible, the key is to mimic the residents. To throw away the guidebooks and instead live like a local, choosing low-key areas to hang out in, and falling into the rhythm of local life.

Visiting congested tourist sites just because everyone else is creates some awful bottlenecks, so making city breaks green in part means tailoring them specifically to you. If you don't like museums or churches, don't visit them. Instead, follow your interests as you would at home, as journalist Elizabeth Becker suggests (see page 17). If you're a passionate foodie, visit food markets and farms to meet local growers; if you love vintage stores, plan a walking tour exploring them.

Certain world cities are inherently greener. Copenhagen, for example, consistently ranks as Europe's greenest city and is aiming to become the world's first carbon neutral city by 2025, while Vancouver has committed to becoming zero-waste by 2040. Travelling to destinations that have banned

single-use plastics, are preserving local culture or have eco-friendly transport means you're voting with your tourist dollar for sustainable cities. Finding alternatives to mass-touristed cities is another way to avoid destructive city travel.

The most sustainable city break of all, however, could be the 'microcation' you take in your own backyard. Spending a weekend exploring your own city or one nearby like a traveller saves time, money and environmental impact, and helps you appreciate your home with fresh eyes. This can make us better custodians of our homes, as well as better ambassadors for our countries whenever we travel abroad.

Plan + Eco-Charge Your Green City Break

Choose Your Destination

Do your research thoroughly to make sure you're staying in the area that's right for you, not just where other tourists are staying. You want to be as close to the things you want to see and do as possible, so you can walk or bike between them.

Getting Around

Walking and biking are the most planet-friendly options. If they're not possible, use public transport. Travelling by train, subway, bus, tram or ferry leads to less traffic and air pollution, gives you a great window into the local culture, and helps you understand the city's layout better.

Eating + Drinking

Look for restaurants that are doing their bit to leave a more positive 'foodprint', favouring those that prioritize SLO food, that place plants at the forefront of their menu and are making attempts to source meat, dairy and fish ethically, and that are creating as little waste as possible. This way, you're cutting down food miles and supporting local producers. Spend time wandering around local markets, and check out the EatWith app to see if there are any locals' homes you could eat in where you are.

Workshops + Talks

Look for workshops on fermentation, foraging, candle making or sustainable building, or talks on electric vehicles, green beauty and lifestyle, zero-waste living or sustainable fashion – skills that will improve your life back home.

Staying

Prioritize small, locally owned hotels rather than big international chains, properties using solar or wind power or finding innovative ways to reduce energy demands, vegan hotels, and those built using natural raw materials. Also consider house-sitting, house-swapping and homestay or couch-surfing options.

Packing

Aside from your 'capsule wardrobe' of basics and simple colours – including a great pair of walking shoes, light layers, a good jacket and a cross-body bag or backpack – carry a reusable food container for takeaway meals or leftovers and your water bottle.

Adventuring

Try avoiding group tours and planned itineraries in favour of being a *flâneur*, strolling the city streets aimlessly, sitting at cafés watching locals interact and allowing the place to reveal itself to you slowly. Remember: the best thing on your itinerary is usually the one that's not on it.

Packing List

This list of 20 products, while by no means exhaustive, will help you minimize your waste and energy consumption on the road and help you pack lighter, so you can maximize every minute of your precious travel days. Brands mentioned are a guide only; always try to opt for local products that don't require shipping if possible.

Zero-Waste Essentials

1. Reusable water bottle

Choose a double-insulated one that can double as a cup for hot drinks or soups. Swell. com has a huge range of styles and colours in stainless steel and their bottles keep drinks hot for 12 hours and cold for 24, while the livelarq.com bottle self-cleans and purifies water using an inbuilt UV light, making it perfect for outdoor adventures.

2. Bamboo cutlery + straw

You'll never have to accept a disposable plastic utensil again. Bambaw.com sell sets with everything needed (fork, knife, spoon, straw) and their products are shipped CO_2 neutrally and are packed plastic-free.

3. Food container

A stainless-steel, bamboo or silicone container is great for storing leftovers from restaurants, and for packing healthy lunches and snacks. Black-blum.com have a leakproof, stainless-steel option that's oven- and freezer-safe.

4. Organic linen or hemp tote

For groceries, collecting trash as you travel, dirty laundry or simply as a day bag. Remember to try to avoid water-intensive cotton.

5. Handkerchief and face mask

An old-school hanky means you can refuse paper napkins and tissues, plus it can be used instead of a disposable wet wipe for freshening up. You can usually find lots at your local thrift store. With facial coverings often mandated in public places, an eco-friendly, reusable cloth mask is another must-pack – look for hand-dyed hemp and organic cotton masks, with slits to insert filters.

6. Quick-dry towel

So you can avoid using hotel towels, which are often washed far more frequently than necessary; especially useful if you're staying only one night.

Mindful Must-Haves

7. Recycled-paper journal

To help you stay clear and calm on the road (refer to page 78 for journalling prompts). A sketch pad could also be useful, if you're into drawing or scrapbooking.

8. Analogue camera

To help slow your travels down. Remember what photographer Jimmy Nelson said on page 83? 'The fewer images you take, the greater emotional investment you will put into them.'

Green Garb

9. Travel 'uniform'

A simple travel style means a lighter bag and a more relaxed you. Pack as little clothing as possible; always consider vintage and second-hand first if you need something, or support ethical companies producing quality stuff that lasts if you buy new. One of my favourite brands is ecoalf. com, Spain's first B Corp (certified positive-impact business) fashion brand that makes stylish clothes, bags and shoes from plastic bottles recovered from the bottom of the ocean.

10. Sewing kit

Mend clothes on the go, rather than discarding them.

11. Walking shoes

Maximize the time you spend travelling by foot. If you need to buy new, look for brands using materials such as organic cotton and recycled food waste, and avoid anything using plastics or petroleum. I love what veja-store.com and allbirds.com are doing in the eco-shoe space.

12. Laundry powder + line

Hotel laundries typically wash every guest's clothes separately, so by doing your own laundry in the sink or bathtub, you'll save water. Take the most natural product possible; laundry strips are a good option for travel.

Clean Toiletries

13. Soap + shampoo

BYO, so you can avoid the small plastic bottles hotels usually offer. If it works for your hair, a natural shampoo bar is a lightweight, package-free option – ethique.com do plastic-, palm oil-, cruelty-free bar shampoos and conditioners. Otherwise, humangear.com sell GoToob silicone travel bottles to put your regular products in.

14. Chemical-free everything

Face wash, hand sanitizer, insect repellent, deodorant – always opt for the most natural version, so toxic chemicals don't end up on your body and in waterways. Look out for greenwashing and learn which chemicals to avoid, including parabens, phthalates, PEGs and synthetic fragrances. Also avoid products containing plastic microbeads (illegal in the EU). Exfoliator, I'm looking at you.

15. Reef-safe sunscreen

Common UV-filtering ingredients, like oxybenzone and octinoxate, have been linked to coral bleaching. Look for sunscreens without these ingredients, which are labelled as 'reef-safe' – stream2sea.com is a great option.

16. Metal razor

Instead of throwing more disposable plastics in the bin, opt for a metal razor where only the blades need replacing. I converted to leafshave.com a couple of years ago and haven't looked back.

17. Reusable swabs + makeup wipes

There are now cotton swabs made from reusable silicone, which saves more disposable plastic. But this is only if you feel you absolutely need this, because most of us don't - our ears are actually self-cleaning. Replace disposable makeup wipes with a face washer or reusable, washable makeup remover that cleans and exfoliates your face, such as facehalo.com.

18. Biodegradable toothbrush

About 3.6 billion plastic toothbrushes are estimated to be used worldwide every year, with roughly 80 per cent of them ending up in the sea. Switch to ones made from bamboo or non-GMO corn starch, where only the bristles aren't biodegradable; look at thehumble.co or boobalou.co.uk. Avoid more plastic by switching to biodegradable, non-toxic dental floss. Tampons also create an enormous amount of waste (according to *National Geographic*, American women will throw 10,000 away in a lifetime), so a menstrual cup and period underwear are also excellent investments; see divacupglobal.com.

Adventure Kit

19. Solar charger / power bank

The more you can be off the grid, the better.

20. Sterilization pen

Whether you're in an Indian city or the middle of the woods, a SteriPEN lets you fill your bottle with water from any tap, lake or stream, then sterilize it using a purifying UV light.

About the Author

Nina Karnikowski has been a travel writer since 2012. Based in Australia, she writes sustainability-focused travel stories for newspapers, magazines and websites. Her first book, *Make a Living Living: Be Successful Doing What You Love*, was published in 2020. Learn more at ninakarnikowski.com, or @travelswithnina on Instagram.

Author's Acknowledgements

My deepest thanks to all of the conscious travel heroes who were interviewed for this book: Elizabeth Becker, Ben Bressler, Céline Cousteau, Caitlin Garcia-Ahern, Rob Greenfield, Marit Miners, Beks Ndlovu, Jimmy Nelson, Tanya Streeter and Lisa Vitaris – you are my heroes, thank you for fighting for a better travel future.

Thank you to my first readers: Laetitia Cross, Abi Fincham, Mary Karnikowski, Nathalie Kelley, Nicole Kuepper, Celeste Mitchell, Hannah Silverton, Ellie Waterhouse and Tandi Williams. Your thoughtful feedback and wise counsel helped develop and hone my ideas, and this book is so much richer for it.

Special thanks to my commissioning editor, Zara Larcombe, for believing in this book, especially during such a difficult time for the travel industry. And to my editor Clare Double, for her remarkable attention to detail and sharp ideas. To the rest of the team at Laurence King Publishing, especially Alex Wright, who did such a beautiful job of designing this book. My sincere gratitude goes out to my illustrator Xuan Loc Xuan, whose earthy aesthetic and beautiful woodblock-style work gives this book the uplifting, hopeful tone I always envisaged for it.

To all of my travel editors over the past decade, whose support has allowed me to see the world and to develop my own ideas around how the industry needs to be reshaped – especially to Lauren Quaintance, Anthony Dennis and Fiona Carruthers.

I would also like to thank the writers and activists who have helped shape my sense of stewardship for our fragile planet. Among them are Thich Nhat Hanh, Clover Hogan, Rob Hopkins, Pico Iyer, Naomi Klein, Nikki Reed, Greta Thunberg, Krista Tippett and George Stone. My worldview, and this book, would not exist without your revolutionary ideas.

Finally to my husband, Peter Windrim, for his daily encouragement, support and endless bright ideas, especially for coming up with the title of this book. There's no one whose opinion I place more highly than yours. Thank you for putting up with my extended absences over the years, and for walking this path towards a more regenerative future beside me.

Portrait Photography Credits

Elizabeth Becker (page 16)
by William Nash
Tanya Streeter (page 30)
by Tim Aylen
Marit Miners (page 58)
by Sahul Miners
Rob Greenfield (page 70)
by Sierra Ford Photography
Caitlin Garcia-Ahern (page 122)
by Paula Harding